Debt Stability

How to Reduce Debt Pressure, Regain Control, and Build Long-Term Financial Stability

Mark Ellison

PERENNIAL PUBLISHING

Published by Perennial Publishing

First Edition

Paperback ISBN: 978-1-971996-95-0
Hardcover ISBN: 978-1-971996-96-7
EBook ISBN: 978-1-971996-97-4

For bulk or institutional orders, contact Perennial Publishing.

Contents

Debt as Financial Pressure, Not Personal Failure

Debt is usually discussed as a number.

A balance owed. A monthly payment. An interest rate. A payoff timeline.

But households rarely experience debt as mathematics alone.

They experience it as pressure.

A payment arrives before income feels ready. A balance remains active despite months of effort. A repair becomes another obligation instead of a temporary disruption. Minimum payments preserve order without restoring flexibility. Income arrives already partially assigned before the month has fully begun.

Over time, debt changes the way a household operates.

Future income becomes increasingly committed in advance. Liquidity becomes harder to rebuild. Timing grows more important. Ordinary disruptions become more difficult to absorb cleanly. The structure becomes more dependent on uninterrupted continuity because less flexibility remains available underneath recurring obligations.

This is why debt often feels heavier than the balance itself.

The balance matters. But the pressure surrounding the balance frequently matters more.

Debt becomes destabilizing when it reduces the household's ability to absorb ordinary life.

That idea forms the foundation of this book.

Debt Stability approaches debt not as a moral issue, but as a structural condition. The purpose of this book is not to separate "good" households from "bad" ones, nor to frame debt as evidence of discipline, intelligence, or worth. Most debt systems do not emerge from a single reckless decision. More often, pressure develops gradually through timing gaps, rising costs, irregular expenses, medical bills, vehicle repairs, income interruptions, thin liquidity, financing structures, and the slow accumulation of recurring obligations across time.

Many households enter debt while trying to preserve continuity rather than expand irresponsibly.

A repair must be handled.

A payment must remain current.

Income arrives late.

Hours fluctuate.

An emergency appears before reserves fully rebuild.

The borrowing itself may be temporary.

The pressure created afterward often is not.

This distinction matters because debt is commonly interpreted too narrowly. Conversations about debt often focus almost entirely on repayment speed, discipline, optimization, or emotional intensity. The assumption becomes that balances disappear primarily through greater effort or stricter behavior.

But debt pressure is rarely explained clearly enough as an operating system.

Debt is financial pressure created when future income becomes committed before the future arrives.

That commitment changes how the household functions.

More income becomes unavailable before it is earned. More coordination becomes necessary. More timing sensitivity develops. More dependence on stable cash flow appears. Financial time compresses because disruptions become harder to absorb without consequences spreading forward into future months.

A household operating under debt pressure therefore experiences more than repayment itself.

It experiences reduced flexibility.

This reduction in flexibility often becomes visible in subtle ways before it becomes visible in dramatic ones.

A delayed paycheck creates more strain than before. An irregular expense disrupts the month more aggressively. A medical bill cannot remain temporary because liquidity is too thin to absorb it directly. Multiple due dates create coordination fatigue. Progress feels fragile because one disruption can erase months of repayment effort quickly.

Even ordinary decisions begin carrying more pressure because less operating margin remains available underneath them.

This is why debt stability cannot be understood solely through balances or payoff timelines.

A household may technically remain current while still operating under severe compression. Accounts may remain open while liquidity weakens steadily. Balances may decline slowly while future obligations continue limiting recovery capacity underneath. Repayment may continue while new borrowing simultaneously reforms through recurring shortfalls elsewhere in the structure.

The issue is not only how much debt exists.

The issue is how much pressure the structure can absorb before instability spreads.

This book was written to make that pressure more visible and more interpretable.

Not to intensify shame.

Not to create panic.

Not to promote financial purity.

And not to turn debt into a moral identity.

Debt Stability is not a payoff challenge, credit repair guide, or repayment-method debate. It is not built around motivational intensity, strict budgeting culture, or financial performance language. It does not assume households become stable through aggression alone. It does not frame ordinary borrowing as personal failure. And it does not promise that one formula or one universal strategy solves every structure equally.

Instead, this book examines how debt pressure forms, spreads, persists, and can gradually weaken over time.

Some of that pressure emerges through obligation load itself. Some through compressed runway and reduced liquidity. Some through payment structures that fit poorly inside real income timing. Some through repeated substitution, where ordinary shortfalls quietly become recurring balances. Some through the gradual expansion of baseline operating costs that reduce future flexibility before instability becomes visible.

Over time, these pressures interact with one another.

A household carrying dense obligations becomes more sensitive to timing disruptions. Thin liquidity increases the likelihood that ordinary instability converts into future debt. Minimum payments may preserve continuity while slowing actual flexibility recovery. Aggressive repayment may destabilize the system if repayment intensity removes too much operating margin underneath it.

This is why the book repeatedly returns to one central idea:

Control returns gradually as pressure decreases.

That process usually does not feel dramatic.

Most households do not wake up one morning suddenly stable. More often, stability returns through reduced fragility.

A repair no longer creates immediate panic.

A delayed expense no longer destabilizes the month automatically.

Timing coordination becomes less exhausting.

Liquidity absorbs more disruption directly.

Fewer dollars are already assigned before income arrives.

The household becomes less dependent on perfect continuity because more flexibility exists underneath ordinary life again.

That gradual return of flexibility matters because debt stability is not simply the removal of balances. It is the rebuilding of a structure capable of absorbing ordinary variability without repeatedly converting disruption into future obligation pressure.

This distinction shapes everything that follows.

The book will examine future obligations, compressed financial time, repayment friction, liquidity failure, recurring shortfalls, cash-flow dependence, sustainable repayment, and long-term prevention. But these ideas are connected by a larger principle underneath them all.

Debt pressure weakens when the household regains enough margin to absorb life without continuously borrowing from the future.

That process does not require perfection.

It does not require permanent intensity.

It does not require shame, panic, or financial extremism.

It requires understanding the structure clearly enough to reduce pressure, restore flexibility, interrupt new debt formation, and gradually rebuild the household's ability to absorb ordinary life without repeatedly borrowing from the future.

Debt Is Not Just a Balance

Most people first encounter debt as a number.

A credit card statement arrives showing a balance. An auto loan displays the remaining amount owed. A student loan account lists a total obligation extending years into the future. A medical payment plan shows a remaining amount still unpaid. Debt appears as a figure on a screen, a line on a statement, or a total attached to an account.

Because of this, debt is commonly understood as a balance problem. The primary question becomes how large the number is. A household with a smaller balance is assumed to be in a stronger position than a household with a larger one. Financial pressure is often interpreted through this same lens. If someone feels strained, the explanation appears simple: the balance is too high.

Balances matter. A household carrying large obligations over long periods may face substantial repayment demands, extended interest costs, and reduced flexibility. Ignoring the size of debt entirely would create an incomplete picture.

But the balance alone does not explain why debt feels heavy.

Two households may owe similar amounts while experiencing completely different levels of pressure. One household may operate with manageable monthly obligations, strong liquidity, and enough flexibility to absorb interruptions without immediate instability. Another may remain under constant strain despite owing less overall because required payments consume too much monthly income, leave little room for disruption, and continuously narrow available choices.

The balance explains how much is owed. It does not fully explain how debt behaves inside the household system.

A balance does not show how much income must be committed every month before current needs can be addressed. It does not show whether payments collide with income timing. It does not show how many obligations are stacked together. It does not show how much interest is continuously being added. It does not show whether the household has liquidity available to absorb temporary disruption. It does not show whether the system contains any room for error.

Debt becomes financially significant not only because money was borrowed in the past, but because income that has not arrived yet is already spoken for.

This changes the way debt must be understood.

A balance sitting on a statement is passive. Obligation is active.

Debt becomes active through required payments. Minimum payments arrive every month. Due dates continue regardless of income timing. Interest accumulates according to account terms, not household convenience. Loan schedules continue forward whether expenses rise, income fluctuates, or emergencies occur. Automatic drafts withdraw funds on fixed dates. Payment expectations remain in place long before the next paycheck arrives.

The household does not encounter debt only when looking at the balance. The household encounters debt when future income must immediately move toward existing obligations before it can be used anywhere else.

This is the central mechanism of the chapter.

Obligation Load is the recurring claim that debt places on future income before that income can be used for current needs, savings, recovery, flexibility, or choice.

Debt is therefore not only a financial quantity. It is a structural demand placed on future cash flow.

Once debt is viewed this way, the meaning of pressure becomes clearer. Pressure is not created only by how much is owed in total. Pressure is created by how much future income has already been committed before the future arrives.

A household earning five thousand dollars per month does not necessarily have five thousand dollars available for present decisions. Some portion of that income may already belong to existing obligations before the paycheck is received. Credit card minimums, auto loan payments, student loans, financed purchases, personal loans, medical payment plans, and other recurring obligations create fixed claims against future income streams.

The remaining income after those claims is what the household can actually direct toward current operations, flexibility, recovery, savings, or unexpected needs.

This distinction matters because financial systems operate through flow, not simply totals.

A household can appear functional on paper while operating under severe obligation pressure in practice. The balances themselves may not immediately reveal instability. The recurring claims against income reveal it much faster.

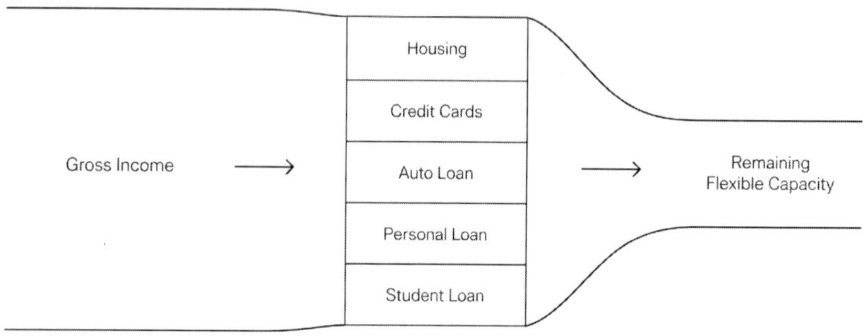

[Figure 1: Debt as Obligation Load]

Once obligations begin stacking together, pressure changes character.

A single payment may appear manageable in isolation. A credit card minimum payment may not seem severe by itself. An auto loan may feel reasonable when viewed alone. A financed appliance purchase may appear small enough to absorb. A personal loan payment may initially fit within the monthly budget without immediate strain.

But household systems rarely contain only one obligation.

Several debts begin layering on top of one another. One due date arrives, then another, then another. Income enters the household already segmented into assigned destinations. A portion moves toward transportation debt. Another portion moves toward revolving credit balances. Another moves toward student loans. Another moves toward medical obligations or financed purchases. What initially appeared manageable individually begins behaving differently collectively.

This is how obligation load accumulates.

Pressure does not rise only because balances rise. Pressure rises because recurring claims against income become denser.

A household carrying multiple moderate debts may experience more instability than a household with one larger obligation structured more manageably. Ten separate obligations with different due dates, interest structures, payment minimums, and account requirements create operational complexity alongside financial pressure. The issue is not merely the total amount owed. The issue is the amount of future income already spoken for every month.

This affects flexibility immediately.

When a larger portion of income has already been assigned to fixed obligations, less remains available for adaptation. Ordinary disruptions become harder to absorb. A temporary reduction in work hours, a medical expense, a vehicle repair, a housing transition, or a timing mismatch between bills and income can create disproportionate stress because the household has limited unassigned cash flow remaining.

Debt therefore narrows the system before a disruption even occurs.

This helps explain an important distinction that is often overlooked: being current is not the same as being stable.

A household may make every payment on time while still operating in a fragile condition. Accounts may remain technically healthy. Bills may continue clearing successfully. No payment may be missed.

But stability depends on more than payment status.

Current means obligations are still being met. Stable means the system contains enough margin to absorb interruption without immediately entering distress.

A household living close to its obligation threshold may appear financially functional right until disruption occurs. The underlying fragility remains hidden because the system has not yet encountered enough pressure to expose it. As long as income arrives exactly as expected and expenses remain within normal range, the structure may continue operating. But the absence of visible failure does not necessarily indicate resilience.

This distinction matters because many households evaluate themselves only through compliance with payments. If accounts remain current, the assumption becomes that the situation is under control. In reality, the system may already be operating with almost no remaining flexibility.

The issue is not simply that debt exists. The deeper issue is that obligation density reduces recovery capacity.

This becomes clearer when debt obligations are compared with more flexible categories of spending.

Some household expenses contain adjustment capacity. Discretionary purchases can often be reduced temporarily. Entertainment spending can shrink. Certain categories of shopping can be delayed. Some lifestyle expenses may expand or contract depending on circumstances.

Debt obligations usually do not behave this way.

Loan payments continue on schedule regardless of whether the month becomes financially difficult. Minimum payments remain due even when other expenses increase unexpectedly. Interest continues accumulating even when income becomes inconsistent. The household may reduce discretionary spending quickly, but debt obligations often remain structurally rigid.

This makes debt behave more like fixed system load than optional consumption.

The distinction is important because flexibility is one of the primary stabilizing forces inside household finance. Flexible systems can adapt under stress. Rigid systems absorb less disruption before pressure begins spreading.

Debt increases rigidity.

Every required payment reduces the amount of income that remains adaptable after income arrives. Over time, this can produce a household structure where large portions of monthly cash flow are permanently committed before new decisions can even be made.

This is one reason debt pressure often feels persistent even when balances are slowly declining. The experience of strain comes less from seeing the total amount owed and more from repeatedly operating inside constrained monthly cash flow conditions.

The household is not only carrying debt historically. It is carrying obligation continuously.

This also explains why debt interacts so strongly with liquidity.

Liquidity represents accessible financial capacity. It provides operational flexibility during disruption, timing mismatches, or uncertainty. A household with available liquidity possesses greater ability to absorb interruption without immediate destabilization.

Debt reduces that flexibility because future income is already allocated elsewhere.

As obligation load rises, the amount of uncommitted income available to build or preserve liquidity tends to shrink. Even households with reasonable income levels may struggle to maintain buffers if recurring obligations continuously consume available cash flow. This creates a reinforcing pressure cycle. Lower liquidity reduces the system's ability to absorb disruption. Reduced absorption capacity increases sensitivity to interruption. Increased sensitivity creates greater dependence on uninterrupted income continuity.

Debt therefore increases income dependence.

When obligation load is high, the household often requires consistent income timing simply to maintain baseline operations. Missing income becomes more dangerous because obligations continue arriving regardless of whether income does. A household with low obligation load may tolerate temporary disruption with manageable consequences. A household with high obligation load may experience immediate instability from even short interruptions because too much future income has already been committed.

This is where debt begins connecting directly to risk exposure.

Risk is not only the probability that something goes wrong. Risk also depends on how much damage the system can absorb when disruption occurs. Obligation load reduces absorption capacity. Less liquidity, less margin, and less flexibility mean smaller disruptions can produce larger effects.

The same event therefore impacts households differently depending on obligation structure.

A temporary income interruption may create inconvenience in one system and severe instability in another. The difference is not always income level. Often the difference is obligation density relative to available margin.

Debt pressure also affects decision capacity.

When households operate with narrow margins, decisions become increasingly constrained by immediate obligations. Short-term payment demands begin dominating financial behavior because required payments cannot easily be delayed. This can reduce the range of available options during periods of uncertainty. Decisions become more reactive because the system contains less time, less liquidity, and less flexibility to evaluate alternatives carefully.

Pressure narrows planning horizons.

A household operating under high obligation load may focus heavily on maintaining immediate continuity because maintaining continuity itself requires significant ongoing coordination. Payment timing, account balances, due dates, and cash flow sequencing begin consuming attention continuously. The issue is not personal failure or lack of discipline. The issue is structural compression.

And importantly, debt does not emerge from a single cause.

Many households accumulate debt gradually through ordinary pressures rather than dramatic financial recklessness. Medical costs, housing transitions, vehicle replacement, temporary unemployment, caregiving responsibilities, education expenses, emergency repairs, income volatility, inflation pressure, or repeated timing gaps between obligations and income can slowly increase dependence on borrowed capacity.

In many cases, debt begins as an attempt to maintain continuity.

A household encounters disruption, insufficient liquidity, or operational shortfall. Credit temporarily fills the gap. Later, another disruption appears before the prior obligation has fully cleared. Over time, recurring obligations accumulate faster than flexibility can recover. What began as isolated borrowing gradually becomes embedded obligation structure.

Understanding this matters because shame often obscures system clarity.

If debt is viewed only as evidence of irresponsibility, the household may focus entirely on guilt while failing to understand the mechanics actually producing pressure. But financial systems cannot be stabilized through emotional judgment alone. Stability requires accurate structural interpretation.

The goal of this book is therefore not to moralize debt. The goal is to explain how obligation pressure behaves, how it spreads through household systems, how it compresses flexibility, and how control is gradually rebuilt over time.

Debt is not simply a number waiting to be reduced.

It is a recurring structural claim on future income.

Once that claim becomes large enough relative to available margin, the household has less flexibility, less liquidity, greater income dependence, and more exposure to disruption.

This is why debt pressure often feels continuous even when balances are technically manageable. The household is not responding only to the total amount owed. The household is responding to the ongoing obligation structure attached to future income.

Understanding debt this way changes the next question entirely.

The issue is no longer only how much is owed.

The issue becomes how much financial time those obligations remove, how quickly pressure spreads when income changes, and how little disruption the household can tolerate before instability accelerates.

That is where the next mechanism begins.

Debt does not only create obligation load. It also compresses financial time and shortens runway.

How Debt Compresses Financial Time

Households often think about money in terms of amounts.

Income is measured in dollars earned. Debt is measured in balances owed. Expenses are measured in monthly totals. Savings are measured in account values. Financial discussions frequently revolve around quantities, percentages, and totals.

But most households experience financial stability through time.

A household with sufficient liquidity, manageable obligations, and operational flexibility usually feels as though it has time to respond when disruption occurs. An unexpected expense may create inconvenience without immediately threatening system stability. A delayed paycheck may require adjustment without creating immediate escalation. Reduced work hours may produce temporary strain without immediately forcing destabilizing decisions.

Another household with similar income may experience the same disruption very differently. Pressure escalates quickly. Available options narrow almost immediately. Decisions become urgent faster. The issue is not always the amount of money involved. The issue is how long the household can continue functioning before financial pressure begins accelerating.

This is why financial stability is closely connected to financial time.

A stable household system usually possesses enough operational time to absorb disruption, adjust gradually, recover from interruption, and continue functioning without immediate destabilization. An unstable system possesses very little time between disruption and escalation.

Debt changes this relationship directly.

Recurring obligations shorten the amount of time a household can continue operating when conditions become difficult. Payments continue moving forward regardless of whether the household is temporarily prepared to support them. This causes debt pressure to behave differently from ordinary spending pressure. Debt obligations do not simply consume money. They consume time.

To understand this clearly, financial runway must first be defined.

Financial runway is the amount of time a household can continue functioning under disruption before obligations begin exceeding available capacity.

Runway is not determined by one factor alone. It is shaped by the interaction between liquidity, recurring obligations, income reliability, expense flexibility, and operational structure.

A household with accessible reserves, manageable fixed obligations, and reliable income timing generally possesses longer runway than a household operating with thin liquidity and dense recurring obligations. A household with lower fixed pressure may tolerate temporary instability for months while adapting gradually. Another may experience severe escalation within weeks because obligations continue arriving faster than recovery can occur.

This is why financial runway matters so much inside household systems.

Runway determines how much disruption can be absorbed before instability begins spreading through the system.

When runway is longer, households usually possess greater flexibility. They have more time to reorganize expenses, replace interrupted income, negotiate operational changes, recover from emergencies, or allow temporary instability to pass without immediate collapse in system function.

When runway is short, adaptation must occur quickly. Decisions become compressed because obligations continue moving forward while available capacity narrows.

Debt directly affects this process because debt obligations remain active regardless of changing conditions.

Minimum payments continue. Loan schedules continue. Interest accumulates continuously. Due dates continue arriving. Automatic drafts continue processing. None of these obligations pause simply because a household encounters temporary instability.

This is the central mechanism of the chapter.

Runway Compression is the reduction of financial time caused by recurring obligations that continue consuming resources during disruption.

Debt compresses runway because recurring obligations reduce how long liquidity, income, and remaining flexibility can sustain operations once disruption begins.

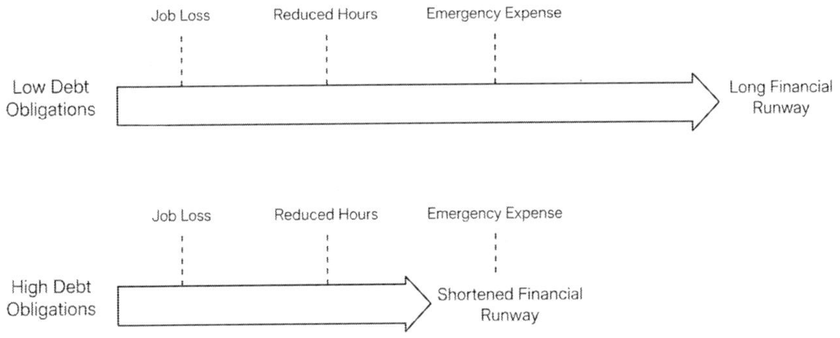

[Figure 2: Debt and Runway Compression]

Once runway becomes compressed, financial pressure accelerates differently.

A household with lower recurring obligations usually possesses more operational flexibility during disruption. If work hours are temporarily reduced, the household may still retain enough available capacity to continue functioning while adjustments are made. If income arrives late, liquidity may bridge the timing gap without immediate destabilization. If an emergency expense appears, the system may absorb the shock while preserving basic continuity.

The disruption still matters. Pressure still increases. But the household possesses time to respond.

Time changes the behavior of financial systems.

A household with greater runway can often evaluate options more carefully, spread adjustments across longer periods, and avoid immediate escalation from temporary instability. The system bends without immediately breaking operational continuity.

Now compare this with a household carrying heavier recurring debt obligations.

The same income interruption produces faster consequences because more incoming cash flow has already been assigned before new conditions are even evaluated. Loan payments remain due. Minimums continue arriving. Existing obligations continue consuming available resources while the household simultaneously attempts to manage the disruption itself.

This reduces recovery time immediately.

The household must solve the problem faster because the structure contains less operational time before pressure begins spreading into other areas of the system.

An emergency expense may begin affecting bill timing more quickly. A delayed paycheck may immediately interfere with required payments. Reduced work hours may rapidly affect liquidity preservation because recurring obligations continue drawing resources away from reserves.

This is one reason debt pressure often feels disproportionately intense during periods of instability. The pressure does not come only from the disruption itself. The pressure comes from the interaction between disruption and compressed runway.

The household is attempting to adapt while the obligation structure continues operating at full speed.

Two households may therefore experience the same external event very differently.

Consider a temporary six-week income interruption.

A household with lower recurring obligations, moderate liquidity, and flexible operating structure may absorb the interruption with manageable adjustments. Spending may tighten temporarily. Certain discretionary activities may pause. Liquidity reserves may decline. But the household retains enough operational space to continue functioning while income recovers or alternative arrangements are made.

The situation is stressful, but the system remains functional.

A household with heavier recurring obligations may encounter immediate compression instead. A large portion of incoming resources was already committed before the interruption occurred. Liquidity begins declining faster because recurring obligations continue consuming cash flow continuously. Available options narrow more quickly because less unassigned income remains available for adaptation.

The disruption itself may not even be larger. The difference is runway duration.

One system possesses more time before instability accelerates. The other possesses less.

This is why debt cannot be evaluated only through balances or interest rates. Debt changes the speed at which pressure spreads through the household system.

Runway compression also explains why liquidity becomes increasingly important under debt pressure.

Liquidity creates temporary operating capacity. Accessible cash reserves, available buffers, and flexible financial resources extend the amount of time a household can continue functioning under instability. Liquidity allows disruption to be absorbed without immediate operational failure.

In effect, liquidity purchases time.

Debt compresses this process because recurring obligations continuously consume resources that might otherwise strengthen liquidity reserves. When obligation load rises, maintaining or rebuilding liquidity often becomes more difficult because available cash flow is already partially committed elsewhere.

This creates a structural tension inside the household system.

Liquidity extends runway. Debt compresses runway.

A household with strong liquidity may temporarily offset some effects of high obligation load because reserves create operational breathing room during disruption. But if recurring obligations remain dense relative to available income, liquidity can erode quickly once instability begins because obligations continue pulling resources away from recovery capacity.

This is why runway matters more than appearance.

Two households may appear similar externally. Both may remain current on payments. Both may maintain similar income levels. Both may possess comparable debt balances.

But the household with greater liquidity, lower recurring obligations, and stronger operational flexibility usually possesses substantially longer runway beneath the surface.

The difference often becomes visible only during disruption.

Timing mismatches illustrate this clearly.

Many household disruptions are not permanent failures. Often they are temporary timing problems. A paycheck arrives later than expected. Contract work becomes irregular for a period. Seasonal income declines temporarily. Expense reimbursements take longer than anticipated. Work hours fluctuate unexpectedly for several weeks.

In systems with adequate runway, these timing irregularities may remain manageable because the household possesses enough liquidity and flexibility to absorb temporary imbalance.

In compressed systems, timing mismatches become much more dangerous.

The issue is not always total income over long periods. A household may technically earn enough money across an entire year while still experiencing severe instability because obligations and income timing do not align consistently enough to preserve operational continuity.

Debt intensifies this problem because recurring obligations usually operate on fixed schedules. Payments arrive according to account structures, not according to the household's preferred timing. When obligation density becomes high, even short income delays can create disproportionate strain because too many claims against future income are already fixed in place.

This increases dependence on uninterrupted income continuity.

As runway compresses, the household often becomes increasingly reliant on predictable income timing simply to maintain normal operations. Interruptions that would once have been manageable begin producing faster instability because the system contains less remaining margin.

Debt therefore changes the household's relationship with uncertainty.

The issue is not necessarily that every disruption becomes catastrophic. The issue is that the tolerance for disruption becomes narrower.

A household with longer runway may absorb temporary instability without major operational consequences. A household with compressed runway may experience immediate strain from relatively ordinary interruptions because too little flexibility remains available inside the structure.

Over time, this affects how the system operates on a practical level.

Planning horizons often shorten under compressed runway conditions because immediate obligations consume more operational attention. Households may focus increasingly on maintaining short-term continuity because recurring obligations leave little room for delayed adjustment.

Stress escalation also accelerates faster under compressed conditions because the system possesses less recovery space between disruption and operational pressure. Problems must be addressed more quickly because runway disappears sooner.

Decision flexibility narrows as well. The household may possess fewer workable options during periods of instability because available resources are already heavily assigned toward existing obligations.

This does not require emotional dramatics to understand. It is simply how compressed systems behave.

A structure with little unused capacity becomes more sensitive to interruption than a structure containing wider margins and longer operational runway.

This connects directly to the broader Money Stability framework.

Liquidity extends runway because accessible reserves create time between disruption and escalation.

Reliable income stabilizes runway because consistent inflow reduces sensitivity to timing irregularities and temporary interruption.

Lower fixed obligations preserve runway because fewer recurring claims against income leave more flexibility available for adaptation.

Risk exposure becomes more significant under compressed runway conditions because the system possesses less ability to absorb unexpected events without destabilization.

Governance also matters because runway compression often develops gradually rather than suddenly. Small recurring obligations added over time may not appear individually severe. A financed purchase here, another payment there, another recurring obligation added quietly into the system. Each obligation slightly reduces available flexibility. Over time, the cumulative effect may substantially shorten operational runway without the household fully recognizing how much recovery capacity has disappeared.

This is one reason debt pressure can feel confusing.

A household may not immediately understand why ordinary disruptions now create disproportionate instability compared to earlier periods. Income may not have collapsed. Expenses may not have changed dramatically. Yet the system reacts more aggressively to interruption than it once did.

Often the difference is runway duration.

As recurring obligations accumulate, the amount of time available for adaptation shrinks. Pressure spreads faster because the household possesses less operational space between disruption and instability.

Understanding this changes the way debt must be evaluated.

The question is not only how much debt exists.

The question is how much time the obligation structure leaves available once disruption begins.

A household with manageable runway may continue functioning through instability with enough flexibility to recover gradually. A household with compressed runway may experience accelerating pressure from relatively ordinary disruptions because obligations continue consuming resources faster than recovery can occur.

Debt therefore affects more than monthly cash flow.

It affects the system's tolerance for interruption.

It affects recovery speed.

It affects liquidity preservation.

It affects the amount of time available for adaptation before pressure begins spreading through the household structure.

But not all debt creates the same level of instability.

Some obligations remain manageable relative to income, liquidity, and operational flexibility. Others create destabilizing pressure because the obligation structure overwhelms available margin and compresses runway too aggressively.

Manageable Debt vs. Destabilizing Debt

Debt is often evaluated through balances.

A household carrying a large mortgage, student loan balance, or business-related obligation may appear financially vulnerable simply because the total amount owed is substantial. Another household carrying smaller balances may appear safer because the numbers seem more contained.

But balances alone do not fully determine instability.

A larger debt load may remain manageable inside a household structure with predictable income, sufficient liquidity, moderate fixed expenses, and enough flexibility to absorb recurring payment obligations without disrupting overall stability. At the same time, a much smaller debt load can become destabilizing if recurring payments consume too much of the household's available margin.

This is one reason debt discussions often become oversimplified.

The conversation is frequently reduced to categories such as "good debt" versus "bad debt," or debt versus debt-free living, as though financial stability can be explained entirely through labels. But household financial systems do not behave according to simple ideological categories. The same obligation may remain manageable in one structure and destabilizing in another depending on how recurring payment pressure interacts with liquidity, income consistency, fixed expenses, and operational flexibility.

The deeper issue is not only how much debt exists.

The deeper issue is how much recurring payment pressure the household can absorb while continuing to function normally.

This is the mechanism that matters most.

Payment Tolerance Range is the amount of recurring payment pressure a household can absorb while preserving operational flexibility, liquidity, recovery capacity, and financial continuity.

The emphasis here is on absorption capacity.

A stable household does not necessarily avoid all debt. Stability depends on whether recurring obligations fit inside the household's available margin without continuously narrowing flexibility or reducing recovery capacity.

Some households can carry recurring obligations without major operational strain because enough stabilizing factors exist elsewhere in the structure. Income may arrive consistently. Liquidity reserves may provide operational buffers. Fixed expenses may remain manageable relative to cash flow. Margin may exist between required obligations and available income. Temporary disruptions may be absorbed without immediately destabilizing the system.

In those situations, debt obligations remain inside the household's tolerance range.

The obligations still matter. Payments still reduce available income. But the recurring pressure remains absorbable without forcing continuous adaptation or eroding long-term stability.

Other households operate much closer to obligation thresholds.

The issue is not always dramatic overspending or obvious financial collapse. Often the structure simply contains too little remaining flexibility once recurring obligations are paid. Most incoming income is already assigned before new decisions are made. Small disruptions begin producing larger effects because the household possesses little unused capacity.

This is where debt becomes destabilizing.

The destabilization may not appear immediately visible from the outside. Payments may still be current. Accounts may still appear operational. Bills may continue clearing successfully.

But technical payment compliance can create misleading signals.

A household may remain current while operating under severe financial strain.

This distinction matters because "current" and "stable" are not the same condition.

Current means required obligations are still being paid according to schedule.

Stable means the household can continue meeting obligations while preserving liquidity, flexibility, and recovery capacity under ordinary disruption.

Resilient goes further still. A resilient household can absorb larger instability, recover gradually, and maintain continuity without immediate structural breakdown.

These are different levels of financial condition even if outward payment behavior initially looks similar.

A household may remain current while steadily draining liquidity reserves, delaying maintenance, carrying balances longer than before, relying on future income expectations to bridge gaps, postponing medical expenses, narrowing spending flexibility, or continuously managing timing pressure between obligations and income arrival.

From the outside, the household appears functional because no payment has technically failed.

Underneath, tolerance range may already be deteriorating.

This is one reason financial strain often develops gradually rather than suddenly.

Most destabilized systems do not collapse overnight. More commonly, the household slowly adapts to rising recurring pressure over time. Savings contributions shrink first. Then liquidity stops rebuilding after emergencies. Small balances remain unpaid longer. More income becomes committed before the month begins. Flexibility narrows gradually rather than dramatically.

The system continues functioning, but with declining recovery capacity.

Eventually, ordinary disruptions begin creating outsized consequences because the household is already operating near its payment threshold.

This threshold differs from one household to another because payment tolerance depends on multiple interacting conditions.

Income consistency matters because predictable income stabilizes recurring obligations. A household with highly reliable income timing can usually absorb recurring payments more easily than a household with irregular contract work, seasonal fluctuations, or variable hours.

Liquidity reserves matter because accessible savings create operational breathing room during temporary instability. Liquidity allows recurring obligations to remain manageable during interruptions that would otherwise create immediate pressure escalation.

Fixed expense load matters because debt obligations do not exist in isolation. Housing costs, utilities, insurance, transportation, childcare, medical expenses, and other recurring operating demands all compete for the same income stream. A debt payment that once felt manageable may become destabilizing if fixed living costs rise significantly elsewhere in the system.

Expense flexibility matters because adaptable systems can absorb disruption more effectively than rigid ones. Households with little adjustable spending capacity often experience faster instability under recurring payment pressure because fewer operational adjustments remain available.

Recovery margin matters because households need enough remaining capacity after obligations are paid to rebuild liquidity, absorb disruption, and maintain continuity over time.

All of these factors influence payment tolerance range simultaneously.

This is why the same payment structure may feel manageable during one period and destabilizing during another.

Tolerance ranges are dynamic rather than fixed.

A car payment that fit comfortably within a household budget during stable income conditions may become much more difficult after housing costs increase, insurance premiums rise, or work hours decline temporarily.

A credit card minimum payment that once appeared manageable may become destabilizing after an illness interrupts income or emergency expenses reduce liquidity reserves.

Several small obligations may each appear individually reasonable while collectively eliminating most remaining monthly flexibility.

This cumulative effect matters more than isolated obligations viewed separately.

A household carrying one larger but predictable obligation may retain more stability than a household carrying many smaller recurring payments spread across multiple accounts, due dates, and financing arrangements. Recurring payment density often compresses flexibility more aggressively than balance size alone.

Each obligation creates another fixed claim against future income.

One payment may not create significant instability. Five or six moderate recurring obligations operating simultaneously can change the behavior of the entire household structure. Timing pressure increases. Margin narrows. Liquidity becomes harder to rebuild. Small disruptions spread faster because too many resources are already committed before the month begins.

This is where payment tolerance range begins shrinking under stress.

Stable conditions can temporarily mask narrow tolerance ranges because ordinary income flow continues supporting the obligation structure. But stress changes the relationship between obligations and available capacity.

Reduced work hours narrow income inflow.

Inflation pressure raises fixed operating costs.

Illness disrupts both income and expenses simultaneously.

Caregiving responsibilities reduce flexibility and available time.

Emergency expenses consume liquidity reserves that once protected the system.

Variable income becomes more difficult to coordinate against fixed due dates.

As flexibility narrows, the same recurring obligations begin consuming a larger share of remaining capacity.

The payment structure itself may not have changed. The tolerance range changed around it.

This distinction is important because households often misinterpret instability as a problem of personal discipline rather than changing structural conditions.

A household may wonder why obligations that once felt manageable now create constant pressure even though total balances have not increased dramatically. In many cases, the answer lies in reduced tolerance range rather than sudden irresponsibility.

The structure lost flexibility.

Liquidity declined.

Fixed costs increased.

Income variability rose.

Recovery capacity narrowed.

As these stabilizing conditions weaken, recurring obligations consume proportionally more operational capacity than before.

This is why ordinary disruptions become more dangerous once systems approach obligation thresholds.

A temporary reduction in hours may not matter much in a household with strong liquidity and wide margin. The same disruption may create immediate timing stress in a household already operating near payment limits.

An emergency vehicle repair may remain absorbable in one structure while forcing revolving balance expansion in another.

A delayed paycheck may create inconvenience in one household and cascading payment pressure in another.

The issue is not always the disruption itself.

The issue is how close the system already operates to its payment tolerance boundary before disruption occurs.

This explains why many financially strained households continue functioning outwardly long after underlying fragility has increased substantially.

The household adapts incrementally.

Savings rebuilding slows.

Maintenance gets delayed.

Small balances linger longer.

Discretionary flexibility disappears.

Timing pressure becomes constant.

Liquidity recovery weakens after every interruption.

The structure remains technically operational, but the range of absorbable disruption becomes progressively smaller.

Eventually, even modest instability begins producing disproportionate strain because the household no longer possesses enough remaining flexibility to absorb ordinary variation.

This also explains why payment pressure often feels exhausting even when no formal crisis exists.

The system may require continuous coordination simply to preserve normal continuity. Due dates, minimums, payment timing, account balances, and income sequencing begin demanding constant operational attention because margin has narrowed too far.

The household is not necessarily collapsing.

But it may be operating with very little tolerance remaining.

This chapter therefore reframes debt stability away from simplistic categories.

The critical distinction is not merely debt versus debt-free living.

It is whether recurring obligations remain inside the household's capacity to absorb pressure without continuously reducing liquidity, flexibility, recovery time, or operational continuity.

A household with debt can remain stable if obligations fit within a sustainable tolerance range supported by liquidity, margin, and reliable income flow.

A household with smaller balances can remain unstable if recurring obligations consume too much available flexibility relative to operating conditions.

Understanding this changes how instability must be interpreted.

The issue is not only how much is owed.

The issue is whether the payment structure leaves enough room for ordinary life to continue functioning without constant compression.

This connects directly to the broader Money Stability framework.

Liquidity protects tolerance range because reserves create flexibility during disruption.

Runway compression narrows tolerance range because shorter financial time reduces adaptation capacity.

Fixed obligations reduce adaptability because more future income becomes structurally assigned before conditions change.

Income variability increases instability under dense payment structures because fixed obligations become harder to coordinate against inconsistent cash flow.

Governance matters because unnoticed obligation growth often accumulates gradually. A few additional recurring payments added over time may quietly reduce flexibility long before the household consciously recognizes how narrow the tolerance range has become.

And even debt that initially remains manageable can become more destabilizing over time.

Interest accumulation, repayment friction, fees, delays, and extended obligation duration can slowly increase pressure persistence even without major new borrowing.

Interest, Friction, and Delay

Many households expect debt pressure to improve quickly once spending behavior changes.

A household may reduce discretionary purchases, stop relying on revolving balances as frequently, avoid taking on major new obligations, or begin making payments more consistently. After a period of visible financial strain, these changes often feel like a turning point. The expectation becomes straightforward: if spending pressure slows, debt pressure should begin fading relatively quickly afterward.

But repayment systems often behave more slowly than households expect.

Even when financial behavior improves, debt pressure may continue for long periods because the structure of repayment contains resistance. Balances continue interacting with interest charges, repayment timing, minimum payment structures, fees, and revolving account behavior long after new spending slows.

This can create confusion.

A household may feel as though it is making responsible adjustments while experiencing far less improvement than expected. Payments continue leaving the household every month. Spending may be more controlled than before. New balances may be growing more slowly or not at all. Yet financial pressure remains present. Liquidity still feels difficult to rebuild. Flexibility still feels narrow. Progress appears slower than the effort being applied.

This is not always a sign that nothing is improving.

Often the repayment structure itself is slowing recovery.

Debt does not only create obligation pressure in the present. It also creates resistance against future stabilization because repayment systems continue absorbing resources over extended periods.

This is the mechanism that matters in this chapter.

Accumulation Drag is the slowing effect created by interest, fees, revolving balances, and repayment friction that extends instability timelines even while repayment continues.

The word "drag" matters because repayment rarely behaves like a clean subtraction process.

Households often imagine repayment as a straightforward reduction sequence. Money is paid toward balances, balances shrink steadily, obligations decline, and pressure gradually disappears. In practice, repayment systems often move much more slowly because portions of repayment flow are continuously diverted away from principal reduction.

Interest absorbs part of each payment.

Fees may extend balances further.

Penalties increase obligations after disruptions or delays.

Minimum payment structures can keep balances active for long periods while reducing principal only gradually.

Revolving balances continuously regenerate pressure because interest continues accumulating across time rather than remaining fixed.

This changes how repayment behaves operationally.

A household may make regular payments for months while experiencing only modest reduction in total balance exposure because repayment flow is partially consumed by the structure surrounding the balance itself.

This is especially common with revolving debt.

A revolving balance behaves differently from a fixed declining obligation because the balance remains active continuously while interest accumulates across repayment cycles. Even when no major new purchases are added, the balance may decline slowly if much of the required payment is directed toward interest rather than principal.

Minimum payments intensify this effect.

A household making minimum payments consistently is still meeting obligations. The account remains current. But the balance may remain active for long periods because minimum payment structures often prioritize continuity of repayment rather than rapid principal reduction.

As a result, repayment timelines stretch outward.

The household continues allocating income toward the balance month after month while the actual reduction in principal may feel much smaller than expected.

Interest extends the timeline.

Fees extend the timeline.

Delayed repayment extends the timeline.

Repeated disruptions extend the timeline further.

Over time, this creates the experience many households describe as feeling "stuck."

The household is moving, but slowly.

Payments continue. Effort continues. Financial behavior may improve meaningfully. Yet pressure remains present because the repayment structure itself contains accumulation drag.

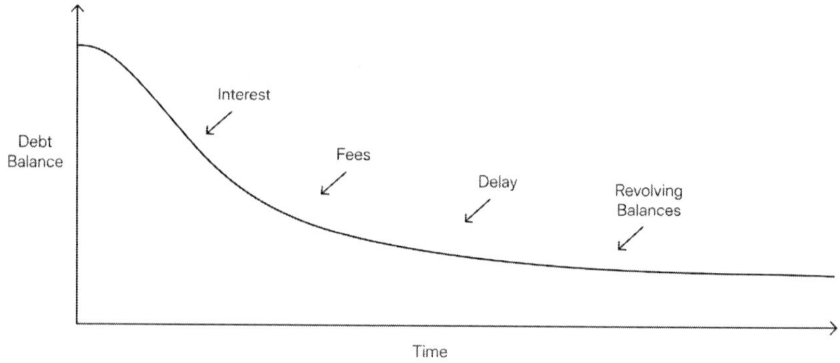

[Figure 3: Interest as Accumulation Drag]

This drag affects more than balances alone.

It affects the household's ability to rebuild stability elsewhere.

Income directed toward long-term repayment obligations is income that cannot simultaneously rebuild liquidity reserves, restore operational flexibility, expand recovery margin, or strengthen runway duration. As repayment timelines extend, more future income remains committed to past obligations for longer periods.

This delays recovery across the entire household structure.

Liquidity rebuilding often becomes particularly difficult under accumulation drag conditions.

A household may want to rebuild emergency reserves after a period of instability, but recurring repayment obligations continue absorbing substantial portions of monthly cash flow. Even when balances slowly decline, liquidity recovery may remain limited because repayment pressure persists continuously.

This creates an important structural tension.

The household may technically be improving while still feeling financially constrained.

Balances may slowly move downward, but operational flexibility may not improve at the same pace because repayment obligations continue consuming resources needed elsewhere in the system.

This helps explain why financial recovery often feels slower than expected.

Households frequently interpret slow improvement as personal failure when the structure itself contains substantial repayment resistance. A person may believe they are doing something wrong because progress feels limited despite visible effort and behavioral change.

But repayment systems are not frictionless.

Interest accumulation alone can significantly slow principal reduction over extended periods. When multiple balances operate simultaneously, this effect compounds. One account absorbs part of the repayment flow through interest. Another balance remains active because minimum payments preserve the obligation across time. A third account expands slightly after an unexpected expense interrupts repayment momentum.

The household continues moving forward, but progress becomes stretched across extended timelines.

This is particularly important because repayment does not occur in isolation from ordinary life conditions.

Disruptions continue occurring during repayment periods.

An emergency vehicle repair may temporarily interrupt repayment progress.

Medical expenses may increase revolving balances again after months of gradual reduction.

Reduced work hours may force the household to prioritize continuity over accelerated repayment.

Timing mismatches between income and obligations may create temporary reliance on revolving credit even after spending behavior has improved overall.

When these interruptions occur, accumulation drag intensifies.

Balances remain active longer.

Interest continues accumulating.

Recovery timelines extend further outward.

Liquidity rebuilding slows again.

This does not necessarily mean the household has failed.

It means repayment systems remain vulnerable to interruption while balances stay active across time.

The longer repayment timelines extend, the longer debt pressure remains embedded inside the household structure.

This is one reason debt instability often resolves gradually rather than quickly.

Even when households improve financial behavior substantially, the effects of prior obligations may continue shaping liquidity, flexibility, and operational capacity for years. The repayment period itself becomes part of the household's financial condition.

During this period, obligations remain active.

Recurring payments continue reducing available cash flow.

Liquidity rebuilding remains slower than desired.

Runway restoration takes longer.

Recovery capacity improves gradually rather than immediately.

The system may become more stable over time while still remaining under continuous repayment pressure.

This prolonged pressure creates another important effect: operational fatigue.

Months of narrow financial margins can become years of constrained flexibility when accumulation drag remains persistent. The household may continue functioning normally on the surface while operating under long-term low-level pressure beneath the surface.

The issue is not dramatic crisis.

The issue is duration.

When repayment timelines stretch across extended periods, the household spends longer operating inside constrained financial conditions. Flexibility remains narrower for longer. Liquidity rebuilding remains incomplete for longer. The ability to absorb new disruption remains weaker for longer.

This increases sensitivity to future instability.

A household carrying extended repayment obligations often possesses less ability to absorb additional disruptions because so much future income remains continuously committed elsewhere. Even moderate instability can interrupt recovery progress because the structure has not yet regained enough flexibility to absorb new pressure easily.

Accumulation drag therefore interacts directly with runway and tolerance range.

Runway restoration takes longer while repayment obligations remain active because recurring claims continue consuming available resources that might otherwise strengthen liquidity or recovery capacity.

Payment tolerance range may narrow over time if obligations persist while flexibility gradually declines elsewhere in the system. Inflation pressure, rising fixed costs, reduced income consistency, or new recurring expenses can slowly reduce the household's ability to comfortably absorb existing repayment structures.

Income reliability also becomes increasingly important during extended repayment periods.

A household with predictable income timing can usually sustain long repayment timelines more steadily than a household with variable hours, seasonal work, or inconsistent contract income. The longer obligations remain active, the more dependent the household becomes on maintaining continuity across those repayment periods.

This is why accumulation drag affects operational confidence as well.

The household may hesitate to rebuild flexibility aggressively because repayment obligations continue remaining present month after month.

Even visible progress can feel fragile if balances still require years of ongoing repayment before meaningful flexibility returns.

Again, this should not be interpreted morally.

Accumulation drag is not evidence of personal weakness. It is a structural characteristic of repayment systems operating across time.

Interest changes repayment speed.

Minimum payment structures extend repayment duration.

Fees and penalties increase resistance.

Revolving balances maintain ongoing accumulation pressure.

Repeated disruptions interrupt momentum and extend timelines further.

All of these conditions affect how quickly households can rebuild liquidity, restore flexibility, and recover operational stability.

This also explains why debt pressure often lingers after the original spending behavior that created the balances has already changed.

The household may no longer be actively expanding obligations in the same way. Spending may be more controlled. Income may have stabilized. Operational awareness may have improved significantly.

Yet repayment pressure remains because existing balances continue generating structural drag across time.

Understanding this matters because households frequently underestimate the duration component of recovery.

The expectation may be that once financial behavior improves, pressure should disappear quickly afterward. But repayment systems often recover incrementally. Progress may remain real while still unfolding slowly because accumulation drag continues extending instability timelines even during periods of improvement.

This chapter therefore reframes debt persistence away from simple behavioral explanations.

The issue is not always ongoing overspending.

Often the issue is that repayment systems continue consuming future income long after the original instability occurred.

Interest extends pressure duration.

Fees extend pressure duration.

Delayed principal reduction extends pressure duration.

Revolving balances extend pressure duration.

Repeated disruptions extend pressure duration further.

As long as obligations remain active, liquidity rebuilding, flexibility restoration, and runway recovery continue moving more slowly than households often expect.

This connects directly to the broader Money Stability framework.

Liquidity rebuilding slows under accumulation drag because repayment obligations continuously absorb resources that might otherwise strengthen reserves.

Runway restoration takes longer while balances remain active because recurring obligations continue compressing operational flexibility.

Income reliability becomes increasingly important during long repayment periods because extended obligations require sustained continuity over time.

Governance matters because unnoticed fees, repayment structures, rates, and revolving behaviors can quietly prolong instability far beyond what households initially expect.

And debt pressure becomes even more destabilizing when repayment obligations fail to align cleanly with income timing and operational cash flow.

Income Mismatch

Many households evaluate financial stability through total income.

If annual income appears sufficient, the assumption often follows naturally: the household should be able to manage its obligations without major difficulty. If enough money is earned across the course of a year, debt pressure may appear explainable only through spending behavior, poor decisions, or excessive borrowing.

But household financial systems do not operate only through totals.

They operate through timing.

Income may be technically sufficient across long periods while still failing to align properly with the timing structure of recurring obligations. A household can earn enough money overall while continuously experiencing operational instability because cash flow does not arrive when obligations require it.

This distinction becomes especially important once debt obligations enter the system.

Debt payments usually operate on fixed schedules. Due dates remain consistent. Minimum payments remain active. Automatic drafts continue processing regardless of changing conditions. Interest continues accumulating according to account timing rather than household convenience.

Income often behaves differently.

A salaried employee with stable payroll timing may receive predictable deposits on consistent dates every month. But many households operate under less stable income conditions. Hours fluctuate. Contract work pays irregularly. Commission income varies across seasons. Overtime changes unexpectedly. Reimbursements arrive late. Scheduling shifts reduce expected inflow temporarily. Freelance payments move inconsistently across weeks or months.

The issue is not always low income.

Often the issue is that rigid obligations collide with variable income flow.

This creates the mechanism that matters in this chapter.

Flow Misalignment is the instability created when repayment obligations do not align with the timing, reliability, or variability of household income flow.

Flow misalignment changes how debt behaves operationally.

A household may technically possess enough income to meet obligations over a monthly or annual period while still experiencing recurring instability because obligations and income arrive on incompatible schedules.

This creates timing pressure.

A payment becomes due before income arrives.

Several obligations cluster within the same week while inflow arrives later.

An expected contract payment gets delayed temporarily while automatic drafts continue processing normally.

Variable work hours reduce expected inflow during a period where obligations remain unchanged.

The household is not necessarily unable to meet obligations in total. The problem is that the timing structure requires tighter coordination than the income structure can consistently support.

This is why financial instability often emerges even without dramatic overspending.

The household may repeatedly experience short-term strain because obligations remain fixed while income behaves unevenly.

Debt intensifies this pressure because debt obligations are usually less flexible than ordinary spending categories. Loan payments continue according to schedule. Minimums remain active. Interest accumulates across delays. Payment structures continue moving forward even when household income timing temporarily weakens.

This creates repeated coordination demands.

A household may shift payment sequencing continuously in order to maintain continuity. One payment is delayed slightly until another paycheck arrives. A revolving balance temporarily absorbs short-term timing pressure. Liquidity reserves decline because income arrives later than expected. Savings rebuilding gets postponed again because current inflow must first stabilize immediate obligations.

None of these conditions necessarily indicate severe financial collapse.

But together they create recurring operational instability.

This is one reason many households feel persistent pressure even when income appears reasonable on paper. The issue is not simply how much income exists. The issue is whether the timing structure of that income aligns reliably enough with recurring obligations to preserve continuity without constant coordination strain.

Flow misalignment becomes more severe as recurring obligation density increases.

A household with relatively few fixed obligations may absorb timing irregularities without major disruption. If one paycheck arrives slightly late or work hours decline temporarily, the household may possess enough flexibility and liquidity to continue functioning normally while conditions stabilize.

A household carrying dense recurring obligations operates differently.

Every fixed payment creates another coordination point. Housing costs, auto loans, credit card minimums, student loans, insurance drafts, medical payment plans, and financed purchases all compete for available inflow.

according to predetermined schedules. The more obligations operating simultaneously, the more precise the timing coordination must become.

This increases operational fragility.

A small delay that would remain manageable in a lower-obligation structure may produce immediate sequencing pressure in a dense obligation structure because too many fixed claims are competing against variable inflow timing.

This is especially visible in households with inconsistent income patterns.

Seasonal workers may experience periods of strong inflow followed by weaker months where obligations remain unchanged.

Commission-based earners may encounter irregular payment timing despite producing adequate annual income overall.

Freelance or contract workers may wait weeks for invoices to clear while recurring obligations continue arriving normally.

Workers dependent on overtime may experience instability when scheduling patterns change unexpectedly.

Households relying on reimbursement structures may temporarily carry obligations while waiting for delayed repayment from employers or institutions.

In all of these situations, the issue is not always insufficient earnings over long periods.

The issue is flow coordination.

Rigid obligations require stable timing.

Variable income often cannot guarantee stable timing consistently.

When these two conditions collide, debt pressure increases substantially.

This interaction also intensifies the mechanisms introduced earlier in the book.

Flow misalignment increases runway compression because timing instability consumes liquidity faster. When income arrives unpredictably, households often draw down reserves simply to maintain continuity between inflow periods. Financial runway shortens because liquidity is repeatedly used to bridge operational timing gaps.

Flow misalignment also strains payment tolerance range. A recurring payment structure that feels manageable under predictable income conditions may become destabilizing once inflow becomes irregular or delayed. The obligations themselves may not change, but the household's ability to coordinate them reliably weakens.

Accumulation drag intensifies as well.

A delayed payment may increase interest accumulation. A revolving balance may remain active longer because temporary timing pressure interrupts repayment momentum. Liquidity rebuilding slows because available reserves are repeatedly redirected toward immediate sequencing needs rather than long-term stabilization.

Over time, these effects compound.

A household experiences timing pressure repeatedly.

Liquidity weakens gradually.

Balances revolve longer.

Interest extends repayment timelines.

Recovery margin narrows.

The household becomes increasingly dependent on precise coordination simply to maintain ordinary continuity.

This is one reason flow misalignment can create ongoing instability even without dramatic financial events.

The household may not be experiencing catastrophic income collapse. Instead, the system may be operating with persistent timing friction that slowly erodes flexibility across time.

A delayed payment here.

A delayed reimbursement there.

Reduced hours for several weeks.

An unexpected expense during a low-income period.

A contract payment arriving later than expected.

Individually, these disruptions may appear manageable. But repeated timing mismatch prevents the household from rebuilding margin effectively because operational attention remains focused on short-term sequencing instead of long-term stabilization.

Liquidity plays an important stabilizing role in this environment.

Accessible reserves create temporary alignment capacity between obligations and delayed inflow. Liquidity allows the household to continue functioning when income timing becomes inconsistent because reserves bridge the gap between due dates and incoming cash flow.

In effect, liquidity smooths timing irregularity.

A household with adequate reserves may tolerate delayed income with relatively limited disruption because obligations can continue being met while waiting for inflow timing to normalize.

Without liquidity, timing sensitivity increases dramatically.

The household may rely on revolving balances temporarily to maintain continuity. Payments may be shifted repeatedly between cycles. Expected future income becomes increasingly important because present obligations still require immediate coordination.

This creates a subtle but important form of instability.

The household may technically remain current on obligations while continuously operating under timing pressure beneath the surface.

The issue is not simply debt itself.

The issue is that the repayment structure requires more timing precision than the income structure can consistently deliver.

This increases operational fatigue over time.

Due-date management becomes constant.

Payment sequencing requires ongoing attention.

Cash flow coordination dominates household financial behavior.

Timing pressure remains active even during otherwise stable periods because the system contains little room for irregularity.

This kind of strain is often misunderstood because it does not always appear dramatic externally.

Accounts may remain current.

Income may appear reasonable annually.

The household may continue functioning normally in outward terms.

Yet internally, the structure may require continuous coordination effort simply to avoid short-term instability.

This is why flow misalignment often creates cumulative instability gradually rather than suddenly.

The household spends increasing amounts of time reacting to timing pressure instead of rebuilding flexibility.

Liquidity recovery slows.

Runway restoration weakens.

Operational margin remains narrow.

Future disruptions become harder to absorb because reserves are repeatedly consumed bridging short-term gaps.

Eventually, even modest irregularities may create outsized effects because the system has lost too much remaining coordination flexibility.

This dynamic also explains why stable income timing often matters as much as total income size.

A household with somewhat lower but highly predictable income may operate more stably than a household with higher but highly irregular income if recurring obligations require tight sequencing coordination.

Predictability stabilizes repayment structures because obligations can be aligned more reliably against expected inflow timing.

Variability increases coordination pressure because obligations remain fixed while inflow shifts unpredictably.

Again, this should not be interpreted morally.

Variable income does not represent personal failure. Many industries and occupations naturally produce inconsistent income patterns. Seasonal employment, commission structures, freelance work, overtime dependency, contract labor, and irregular scheduling exist across large portions of the economy.

The issue is structural compatibility.

Debt obligations prefer consistency.

Income systems often contain variability.

When the variability exceeds the structure's coordination capacity, instability begins spreading through the household system.

This is why governance matters under debt pressure.

Obligation timing structures require active monitoring because small sequencing problems can create larger downstream effects when liquidity is thin and recurring obligations are dense. A household may technically possess enough long-term income while still operating under continuous short-term coordination pressure if timing structures remain poorly aligned.

Understanding this changes the way instability must be interpreted.

The issue is not always that the household lacks enough income overall.

The issue is that the income flow and obligation flow are operating on incompatible timing structures.

Debt pressure therefore emerges not only from balances or repayment amounts, but from sequencing friction between rigid obligations and variable inflow.

This chapter reframes debt instability away from simple income totals.

Financial stability depends not only on how much money enters the household across time, but on whether that inflow arrives consistently enough, predictably enough, and flexibly enough to support the obligation structure attached to it.

When flow misalignment persists, households often begin solving short-term operational gaps through substitution.

Recurring expenses that cannot be absorbed cleanly through current cash flow begin shifting toward borrowed capacity instead.

Expense Leakage and Debt Substitution

Debt often develops gradually.

Many households do not experience a single dramatic financial event that suddenly destabilizes the entire system. There may be no extreme spending episode, no sudden luxury purchase, and no obvious moment where financial control appears to disappear all at once.

More commonly, pressure accumulates through repeated small shortfalls that seem manageable individually but become significant across time.

An irregular bill arrives during a tighter month.

A repair appears before liquidity has fully recovered from a prior expense.

Several recurring costs increase gradually over a year.

A timing mismatch forces temporary reliance on revolving credit.

Small operational gaps begin appearing more frequently than the household can absorb comfortably.

At first, these gaps may feel temporary.

The household expects conditions to normalize after the next paycheck, the next month, or the next period of lower expenses. Borrowed capacity is used briefly to preserve continuity while waiting for operations to stabilize again.

But recurring shortfalls often reappear before recovery fully occurs.

This is how debt substitution frequently begins.

Not through one catastrophic decision, but through repeated operational gaps that slowly become integrated into ordinary household function.

The issue is not necessarily reckless spending.

The issue is that recurring expenses exceed available flexibility often enough that borrowed capacity begins absorbing the difference.

This creates the mechanism that matters in this chapter.

Substitution Pressure is the gradual replacement of operational shortfalls with borrowed capacity when recurring expenses exceed available flexibility often enough across time.

The word "gradual" matters.

Many households do not consciously decide to "live on debt." More often, debt becomes operationally integrated because recurring pressures repeatedly exceed available margin before liquidity can fully recover.

A household encounters a temporary gap.

Credit absorbs it.

Later, another irregular cost appears.

The prior balance remains active while a second shortfall develops.

Then another timing mismatch occurs before savings are rebuilt.

Over time, what began as temporary substitution becomes recurring operational behavior.

This process is often subtle because many destabilizing costs appear small individually.

Expense leakage contributes heavily to this pattern.

Expense leakage does not necessarily mean irresponsible spending or uncontrolled consumption. Often it refers to ordinary recurring costs that gradually reduce available flexibility without receiving much operational attention.

Convenience spending may increase slowly across busy periods.

Automatic renewals continue month after month.

Recurring subscriptions accumulate incrementally.

Administrative fees, delivery costs, service charges, and small recurring purchases spread quietly across categories.

Maintenance costs appear intermittently rather than on predictable schedules.

Household replacement items emerge gradually rather than dramatically.

Individually, none of these expenses may appear large enough to threaten stability.

Collectively, they reduce available margin steadily across time.

This matters because household financial systems depend heavily on remaining flexibility after recurring obligations are paid.

When small recurring costs quietly consume more of that flexibility than expected, operational shortfalls begin appearing more frequently.

The household may still appear financially functional.

Income continues arriving.

Most obligations remain current.

No obvious collapse occurs.

But the remaining margin between incoming resources and outgoing demands narrows gradually until ordinary irregularities become harder to absorb without substitution.

Irregular expenses intensify this process further because many household costs do not arrive on smooth monthly schedules.

Vehicle maintenance appears unpredictably.

Medical expenses fluctuate across periods.

School costs cluster seasonally.

Utility bills rise during extreme weather periods.

Repairs emerge without consistent timing.

Travel obligations, replacement purchases, and administrative expenses often appear intermittently rather than evenly.

These costs are operationally normal, but they create instability when liquidity reserves are insufficient to absorb them cleanly.

In those situations, borrowed capacity frequently becomes the temporary stabilizer.

A revolving balance absorbs the repair.

A financing structure covers the replacement cost.

A credit line bridges the timing gap.

The substitution initially appears manageable because the household preserves continuity without immediate operational failure.

But the obligation remains afterward.

The temporary gap becomes a recurring future claim against income.

Then another irregular expense arrives before the prior obligation has fully cleared.

This is how substitution pressure compounds gradually.

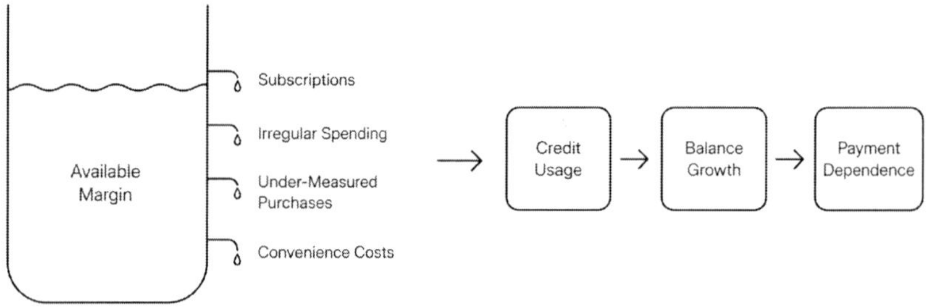

[Figure 4: Expense Leakage to Debt Substitution]

Once substitution patterns begin normalizing, debt starts behaving differently inside the household structure.

A revolving balance originally used for temporary support may become an ongoing coordination tool.

It absorbs delayed income periods.

It bridges irregular expense spikes.

It maintains continuity during tighter months.

It fills short-term gaps while waiting for future inflow.

The household may no longer use borrowed capacity only for extraordinary situations. Borrowed flexibility becomes integrated into ordinary operation.

This distinction matters because it changes the source of debt pressure.

The issue is no longer isolated spending events.

The issue is that ordinary household operation no longer fits cleanly within available flexibility.

The structure itself begins depending on substitution.

This dependence often develops quietly because each individual substitution event appears reasonable in isolation.

A vehicle repair during a difficult month may feel unavoidable.

A temporary revolving balance during reduced work hours may appear manageable.

An irregular expense placed on credit while waiting for delayed reimbursement may seem temporary.

None of these events necessarily indicate severe irresponsibility.

But repeated substitution changes the structure over time.

Each recurring obligation slightly reduces future flexibility.

Less liquidity remains available for future irregularities.

More income becomes assigned before new conditions emerge.

Timing pressure increases because more obligations must now be coordinated simultaneously.

The likelihood of future shortfalls rises because the system contains less remaining margin after existing obligations are paid.

This is where substitution pressure begins interacting directly with the earlier mechanisms in the book.

Obligation load increases because every substituted shortfall becomes another future claim against income.

Runway compresses because recurring obligations reduce how long the household can absorb future disruption before instability accelerates.

Payment tolerance narrows because more recurring payments consume available flexibility.

Accumulation drag intensifies because revolving balances remain active longer while interest extends repayment timelines.

Flow misalignment becomes harder to manage because more fixed obligations now compete against variable income timing.

Each mechanism reinforces the others.

A household experiencing recurring shortfalls substitutes borrowed capacity temporarily.

The substitution creates additional recurring obligations.

Those obligations reduce future flexibility.

Reduced flexibility increases sensitivity to future irregularities.

Future irregularities create additional substitution pressure.

Over time, instability spreads gradually through the structure without requiring one dramatic financial event.

This gradual progression is important because households often adapt slowly to rising substitution pressure.

Balances remain active slightly longer than before.

Savings rebuilding weakens gradually.

Irregular expenses increasingly move toward revolving credit.

Timing pressure becomes more common.

Liquidity recovery slows after disruptions.

Borrowed flexibility begins filling ordinary operational gaps more frequently.

Because these adjustments happen incrementally, the underlying instability may remain difficult to recognize initially.

The household continues functioning.

Bills are mostly paid.

Income continues arriving.

Daily operations continue moving forward.

Externally, the structure may still appear stable.

Internally, the household may be increasingly dependent on borrowed capacity simply to preserve continuity between income periods, irregular expenses, and recurring obligations.

This is one reason debt pressure often feels persistent even without obvious overspending.

The issue is not necessarily dramatic financial behavior.

The issue is that recurring operational demands have gradually exceeded available flexibility often enough that substitution became normalized.

Weak expense visibility intensifies this process.

The problem is not always a lack of budgeting discipline in the conventional sense. More often, the household lacks clear visibility into how much flexibility remains after recurring operational drift accumulates across multiple categories.

Small recurring expenses rarely appear dangerous individually.

Irregular costs often feel temporary rather than structural.

Operational gaps may seem isolated rather than recurring.

Because of this, substitution behavior can continue for long periods before the household fully recognizes how much borrowed capacity has become integrated into ordinary operation.

A household may believe the issue is temporary timing pressure while revolving balances remain active continuously across months or years.

The structure remains operational, but increasingly fragile.

This gradual fragility creates another important effect: reduced recovery capacity.

When borrowed capacity repeatedly absorbs ordinary operational gaps, liquidity becomes harder to rebuild because repayment obligations now compete against current operating costs simultaneously.

The household is no longer only paying for present operation.

It is also paying for past shortfalls that were substituted earlier.

This reduces future adaptability.

An irregular expense that once could have been absorbed through savings may now require additional borrowing because prior substitution obligations already consumed available margin.

Over time, the system becomes increasingly dependent on continuity.

Income timing must remain precise.

Irregular costs become more dangerous.

Disruptions spread faster because flexibility has narrowed.

The household spends more effort coordinating operations and less time rebuilding margin.

Again, this should not be interpreted morally.

Most households encounter periods where expenses rise unevenly, liquidity weakens temporarily, or operational shortfalls emerge unexpectedly. Economic conditions change. Costs drift upward. Repairs happen. Timing mismatches occur. Medical expenses appear. Ordinary life contains irregularity.

Substitution pressure emerges when these irregularities occur frequently enough that borrowed capacity becomes the recurring stabilizer instead of temporary liquidity.

This chapter therefore reframes debt accumulation away from simplistic behavioral explanations.

The issue is not always conscious overspending.

Often the issue is that recurring operational gaps slowly shifted toward borrowed capacity because the structure lacked enough remaining flexibility to absorb them directly.

Understanding this matters because debt instability frequently develops through normalization rather than crisis.

A revolving balance remains active a little longer.

An irregular expense moves onto credit temporarily.

Liquidity rebuilding gets delayed again.

Another shortfall appears before recovery completes.

The household adapts gradually until borrowed flexibility becomes embedded inside ordinary operation.

This connects directly to the broader Money Stability framework.

Liquidity buffers reduce substitution dependence because reserves absorb operational irregularities before borrowed capacity becomes necessary.

Runway compression increases sensitivity to recurring shortfalls because less operational time remains available for recovery between disruptions.

Flow misalignment increases temporary substitution pressure because timing gaps often require short-term coordination support.

Accumulation drag extends recovery because substituted balances remain active long after the original shortfall occurred.

Governance matters because unnoticed operational drift often compounds gradually across time without immediate visibility.

And when liquidity reserves fail entirely during disruption, operational shortfalls often move beyond ordinary substitution patterns into emergency debt dependence.

Emergency Debt and Liquidity Failure

Instability is normal inside household systems.

Most households eventually encounter disruption in some form. A vehicle requires repair unexpectedly. A medical expense arrives outside the ordinary operating pattern. Work hours decline temporarily. A major appliance fails. Emergency travel becomes necessary. A childcare arrangement changes suddenly. A storm damages part of the home. An insurance deductible appears during an already strained period.

These events are not unusual exceptions to household operation.

They are part of household operation.

The important question is not whether disruption occurs. The important question is whether the household possesses enough liquidity to absorb disruption directly without converting the instability into future repayment pressure.

This distinction matters because financial systems do not respond to disruption only through the size of the event itself. They respond through absorption capacity.

A household with adequate accessible reserves may experience disruption as temporary instability. The repair is handled. The emergency expense is absorbed. The interruption creates pressure, but the pressure gradually recedes once conditions stabilize.

A household without sufficient liquidity often experiences the same disruption differently.

The expense does not disappear after the emergency passes.

Instead, the disruption converts into recurring debt obligations that remain active long afterward.

This is the mechanism that matters in this chapter.

Shock Conversion is the process through which ordinary financial disruptions become recurring debt obligations because available liquidity cannot absorb the instability directly.

Liquidity functions as a shock absorber.

Accessible reserves allow operational instability to remain temporary. Repairs, timing gaps, emergency costs, and short-term disruptions can be handled without permanently increasing future obligation pressure.

Without liquidity, the household frequently substitutes borrowed capacity immediately because continuity still has to be preserved.

A vehicle breakdown becomes revolving debt.

A medical bill becomes a payment plan.

Temporary unemployment expands existing balances.

Emergency travel moves onto credit.

A plumbing repair becomes financing.

An appliance replacement creates another monthly obligation.

The original disruption eventually ends.

The repayment obligation often continues long afterward.

This distinction is important because the instability itself may last only days or weeks while the repayment structure created through shock conversion remains embedded in the household system for months or years.

A temporary disruption becomes a long-term obligation.

This changes how debt accumulation must be interpreted.

Emergency debt often differs structurally from discretionary borrowing because the household is not necessarily attempting to expand lifestyle consumption or increase spending flexibility. In many cases, the borrowing occurs because ordinary household continuity cannot be maintained without replacing missing liquidity temporarily.

The borrowing is operational rather than expansionary.

The household still needs transportation.

The medical expense still requires payment.

The emergency travel still occurs.

The repair still must be completed.

Borrowed capacity becomes the substitute for reserves that were unavailable when disruption occurred.

This is one reason debt accumulation often cannot be explained fully through spending behavior alone.

Many recurring balances originate from instability events interacting with insufficient liquidity rather than from dramatic consumption decisions.

A household may spend years gradually carrying obligations created by relatively ordinary disruptions:

a deductible during a medical event, a transmission repair, several weeks of reduced work hours, emergency childcare costs, a roof repair after storm damage, or temporary relocation expenses during instability.

None of these situations necessarily represent financial recklessness.

But when liquidity is thin, ordinary instability frequently converts into future obligation pressure automatically.

This changes how the household operates afterward.

Once disruption becomes debt, future flexibility narrows because repayment obligations now compete against ordinary operating costs simultaneously. Income that might otherwise rebuild reserves or restore flexibility must instead support obligations created by past instability.

This weakens future shock absorption capacity.

One emergency often reduces the household's ability to absorb the next one.

Liquidity rebuilding slows because repayment obligations remain active.

Future runway shortens because more recurring claims now exist against income.

Payment tolerance narrows because obligations consume a larger portion of available flexibility.

The structure becomes more sensitive to future disruption because less margin remains available after recurring obligations are paid.

This creates a reinforcing cycle.

A household experiences disruption.

Liquidity proves insufficient.

Borrowed capacity absorbs the instability.

New obligations reduce future flexibility.

Reduced flexibility weakens future shock absorption.

Another disruption occurs before reserves fully recover.

Additional borrowing becomes necessary again.

Over time, repeated shock conversion increases obligation density while weakening recovery capacity simultaneously.

This is how households gradually become disruption-sensitive.

The sensitivity often develops slowly rather than dramatically.

At first, a single emergency balance may appear manageable. The household expects repayment to occur gradually while normal operations continue. But another instability event appears before recovery is complete. Then another timing problem emerges during repayment. Liquidity remains thin because repayment obligations slow reserve rebuilding.

The household continues functioning, but with declining ability to absorb irregularity.

Eventually, even modest disruptions begin creating disproportionate strain because too much future income is already committed to prior instability events.

This process connects directly to the earlier mechanisms in the book.

Obligation load increases because every converted shock becomes another recurring claim against future income.

Runway compresses because obligations reduce how long the household can operate under future instability before escalation begins.

Payment tolerance narrows because more recurring obligations compete against existing income and expenses.

Accumulation drag intensifies because repayment timelines extend across longer periods while balances continue generating interest or fees.

Flow misalignment becomes harder to manage because additional obligations increase coordination pressure against variable or delayed income.

Substitution pressure also grows because future shortfalls become more likely once reserves remain weak and recurring obligations consume greater portions of cash flow.

Each shock conversion therefore extends instability beyond the original event itself.

This is one reason debt pressure often feels disconnected from present circumstances.

A household may currently be operating relatively responsibly while still carrying obligations created by earlier disruptions. The present structure reflects not only current behavior, but also the accumulated effects of prior instability that could not be absorbed directly when it occurred.

The long-tail nature of shock conversion matters here.

The disruption itself is temporary.

The financial effects often persist much longer.

A temporary illness may create payment obligations that remain active for years afterward.

Several months of reduced work hours may generate balances that continue affecting liquidity long after income stabilizes again.

An emergency repair may narrow flexibility across multiple future periods because repayment obligations reduce recovery capacity afterward.

The original instability passes.

The obligation remains embedded inside ordinary operation.

This helps explain why many households underestimate the importance of liquidity in debt formation.

Debt is often interpreted primarily through the lens of spending decisions, but many balances originate from failed shock absorption rather than intentional expansion of consumption.

The household did not necessarily choose greater financial pressure voluntarily.

The household lacked enough accessible reserves to prevent temporary instability from becoming future obligation pressure.

This distinction becomes especially important during repeated exposure to ordinary disruption.

A household may partially recover after one emergency, but before liquidity fully rebuilds, another instability event appears:
another vehicle repair, another deductible, another temporary income interruption, another irregular expense cluster.

Each event weakens recovery further because the system never fully regains its previous flexibility before absorbing the next disruption.

Over time, recovery periods become shorter while repayment periods become longer.

The household spends increasing amounts of time carrying obligations created by past instability.

This creates operational fatigue.

The household may begin operating defensively because disruption sensitivity has increased substantially. Maintenance may get delayed because reserves feel too thin to absorb additional instability. Irregular expenses begin generating anxiety because prior emergencies already reduced flexibility significantly. Liquidity rebuilding may feel difficult because repayment obligations continue consuming available margin.

The structure remains technically functional.

Bills may remain mostly current.

Income may continue arriving consistently.

Yet beneath the surface, the household may be operating with elevated instability because reserves remain weak while obligations remain dense.

This kind of fragility is often difficult to recognize externally.

A household carrying emergency debt may appear operationally stable because normal continuity continues. But the system's ability to absorb additional disruption may already be substantially weakened.

This is why liquidity should not be understood merely as "saved money."

Liquidity represents operational resilience.

It creates adaptation capacity during instability.

It creates time between disruption and escalation.

It allows ordinary shocks to remain temporary rather than becoming recurring obligations.

Without liquidity, the household becomes increasingly dependent on borrowed capacity to preserve continuity during instability periods.

And once borrowing repeatedly absorbs shocks, future resilience weakens because repayment obligations reduce the system's ability to rebuild flexibility afterward.

Again, this should not be interpreted morally.

Most households eventually encounter periods where reserves prove insufficient relative to operational instability. Medical expenses occur unexpectedly. Vehicles fail at inconvenient times. Work interruptions happen. Deductibles cluster with other obligations. Childcare arrangements change suddenly. Repairs emerge without warning.

The issue is structural exposure, not personal weakness.

Shock conversion simply explains what happens when disruption arrives before sufficient recovery capacity exists.

This chapter therefore reframes emergency debt away from simplistic behavioral explanations.

The issue is not always uncontrolled consumption or reckless borrowing.

Often the issue is that ordinary instability encountered insufficient liquidity and converted directly into future obligation pressure instead.

Understanding this matters because repeated shock conversion changes the long-term behavior of household systems.

Liquidity rebuilding slows.

Obligation density rises.

Recovery periods shorten.

Future instability becomes harder to absorb.

The household becomes increasingly sensitive to disruption because too much future income is already committed to obligations created by past emergencies.

This connects directly to the broader Money Stability framework.

Liquidity absorbs shocks directly before they become future obligations.

Runway determines how long recovery can occur before instability escalates further.

Payment tolerance narrows after shock conversion because more recurring obligations reduce future flexibility.

Accumulation drag slows reserve rebuilding because repayment timelines continue consuming resources long after the original disruption ends.

Governance matters because weak liquidity often remains invisible until instability exposes the absence of sufficient shock absorption capacity.

And over longer periods, borrowed capacity can begin shifting from emergency stabilization toward something more embedded.

What originally functioned as temporary support during instability may gradually become integrated into the household's baseline operating structure itself.

Lifestyle Debt and Baseline Drift

Household instability often develops gradually.

Many financially strained households cannot point to one catastrophic decision that suddenly transformed a stable structure into an unstable one. There may be no single purchase large enough to explain the pressure entirely. No dramatic collapse. No obvious moment where the system visibly failed all at once.

Instead, the operating structure slowly changes across time.

A larger vehicle payment replaces an older one.

Housing costs rise after an upgrade or relocation.

Additional subscriptions accumulate gradually.

Convenience services become integrated into ordinary routines.

Financed electronics remain active month after month.

Buy-now-pay-later structures spread purchases across future income.

Recurring monthly services layer on top of one another quietly.

Individually, each change may appear manageable.

Collectively, the structure becomes more expensive to maintain.

This gradual upward movement in normal operating cost is one of the most important forms of instability because it often develops invisibly during periods that otherwise appear financially successful.

The household may earn more than before.

Income may improve.

Career progress may occur.

Lifestyle expansion may feel justified relative to rising earnings.

Yet underneath the visible improvement, recurring obligations slowly increase the amount of income required simply to preserve ordinary continuity.

This creates the mechanism that matters in this chapter.

Baseline Inflation is the gradual increase in a household's normal operating cost caused by recurring obligations and financed lifestyle expansion that reduce future flexibility over time.

The important distinction is that baseline inflation does not refer primarily to temporary spending spikes.

The issue is not occasional discretionary purchases or isolated periods of elevated spending. The issue is that financed upgrades and recurring obligations become embedded into the household's ordinary operating structure.

The larger vehicle payment becomes part of the monthly baseline.

The upgraded housing cost becomes permanent operating load.

Recurring delivery convenience becomes normalized.

Subscription layering continues quietly across categories.

Financed replacement cycles remain active continuously.

Additional services become operationally expected rather than occasional.

Over time, the household's standard cost of functioning rises.

This changes the structure even when the changes appear manageable individually.

Financing accelerates this process because borrowed capacity allows operating costs to expand before equivalent resilience exists to support them comfortably over long periods.

The lifestyle adjusts upward immediately.

Liquidity, recovery capacity, and operational flexibility often adjust much more slowly.

This difference matters because household systems respond not only to income size, but to how much of future income has already been committed before disruption occurs.

As recurring obligations increase, more future income becomes structurally assigned to maintaining the current operating standard.

The household may still feel financially stable during normal periods because the structure continues functioning under ordinary conditions. Income arrives. Obligations are paid. Daily operation continues without obvious breakdown.

But flexibility gradually narrows underneath the surface.

This narrowing often remains difficult to notice because normalization changes perception over time.

What initially felt like an upgrade eventually becomes ordinary expectation.

The upgraded vehicle no longer feels optional after several years.

The expanded subscription environment becomes routine.

Higher convenience spending becomes operationally standard.

The financed furniture becomes part of normal household structure.

The recurring service layers stop feeling like additions and start feeling like the baseline itself.

This is one reason baseline inflation develops quietly.

The household adapts operationally and psychologically to the elevated structure long before instability exposes the reduced flexibility underneath.

And because many periods of baseline expansion occur alongside rising income, the structure can appear sustainable for long stretches of time.

Raises occur.

Income improves.

Housing expands.

Financed obligations increase gradually alongside earnings.

The household may genuinely feel financially stronger than before because consumption capacity increased successfully.

But rising income does not automatically create rising resilience.

Sometimes obligation growth outpaces flexibility growth.

This distinction becomes important only when disruption occurs.

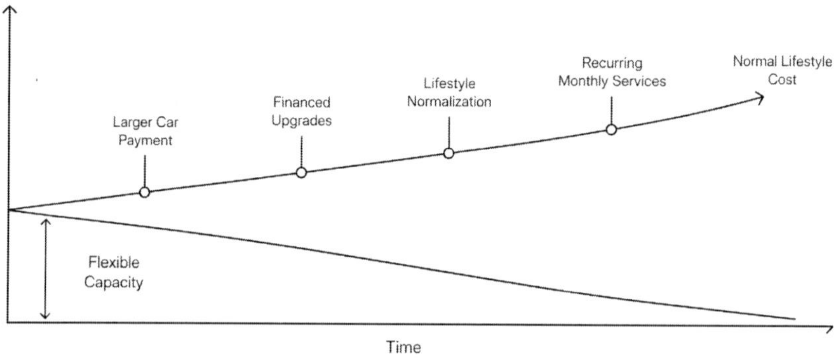

[Figure 5: Baseline Drift and Rising Obligation Load]

A household with lower recurring operating costs usually possesses more adaptability during instability because less income is required simply to preserve ordinary continuity.

Temporary income reductions may remain manageable longer.

Irregular expenses may be absorbed with less coordination pressure.

Liquidity rebuilding may occur more easily because fewer recurring claims compete against available cash flow.

A household with elevated baseline obligations operates differently.

More inflow must remain uninterrupted simply to maintain the current operating structure. More recurring payments compete for future income before new conditions are evaluated. More monthly obligations remain fixed regardless of changing circumstances.

This increases disruption sensitivity substantially.

A temporary reduction in income may create larger consequences because the operating threshold itself became more expensive.

A repair or medical expense may create greater strain because liquidity rebuilding had already weakened under elevated recurring obligations.

Timing disruptions become harder to absorb because more payments now require precise coordination.

The issue is not necessarily excessive luxury or irresponsible spending.

The issue is structural rigidity.

As baseline costs rise, flexibility often declines even if income simultaneously increases.

This explains why some households feel increasingly fragile despite earning substantially more than earlier periods of life.

The higher income improved operating capacity, but the operating threshold rose alongside it.

More income now flows toward preserving the current structure before reserves can rebuild, flexibility can expand, or future disruptions can be absorbed comfortably.

This is one reason financial strain can feel confusing during periods that outwardly appear successful.

The household may possess higher income, larger assets, newer purchases, and upgraded living conditions while simultaneously operating with thinner margins beneath the surface.

Visible expansion does not always indicate operational resilience.

A household may appear externally stable while internally depending heavily on uninterrupted income continuity simply to maintain ordinary operation.

Baseline inflation contributes heavily to this condition because recurring obligation layering changes the system gradually rather than dramatically.

One financing plan may not create major instability.

One subscription may appear insignificant.

One upgraded payment may fit comfortably at the time it is added.

But recurring obligations accumulate structurally.

A larger vehicle payment combines with higher insurance costs.

An upgraded housing payment combines with additional maintenance obligations.

Recurring digital services layer across entertainment, communication, storage, software, and convenience categories.

Financed electronics overlap with appliance replacement cycles.

Buy-now-pay-later obligations distribute smaller purchases across future income periods.

Individually, each obligation may remain manageable.

Collectively, they raise the baseline cost of ordinary life substantially.

This cumulative effect often remains invisible because the changes occur incrementally.

The household adapts gradually to each new obligation before the next one appears. Since no single addition immediately destabilizes the structure, the long-term effect becomes difficult to recognize clearly.

The system continues functioning.

Bills remain current.

Income supports the structure during stable periods.

But flexibility erodes quietly.

Liquidity rebuilding slows because more income is continuously committed elsewhere.

Runway compresses because higher recurring obligations reduce the amount of disruption the system can absorb before escalation begins.

Payment tolerance narrows because the household now operates closer to obligation thresholds.

Accumulation drag intensifies because more financed obligations remain active simultaneously across longer repayment periods.

Substitution pressure grows because irregular costs become harder to absorb cleanly once baseline operating costs consume greater portions of available cash flow.

Shock conversion becomes more likely because reserves rebuild more slowly under elevated recurring obligations.

Each mechanism compounds the others.

And because baseline inflation usually develops gradually, instability may remain hidden for long periods.

A household may continue functioning successfully during stable economic conditions while underlying fragility increases steadily underneath the surface.

This is why disruption often reveals baseline inflation more clearly than ordinary periods do.

During stable income periods, elevated obligations may feel sustainable because inflow continues supporting the structure consistently.

But once instability appears, the reduced flexibility becomes much more visible.

A temporary reduction in hours suddenly matters more because the operating threshold is higher.

An irregular expense creates greater strain because liquidity reserves remained thinner than expected.

A timing disruption becomes harder to coordinate because more recurring obligations require precise sequencing.

The household discovers that maintaining ordinary operation requires more continuity than before.

Again, this should not be interpreted morally.

The issue is not whether households "deserve" comfort, upgrades, convenience, or improved living conditions. Many financed purchases genuinely improve quality of life, operational efficiency, or household functionality.

The issue is structural exposure.

Every recurring obligation slightly increases the amount of future income required simply to preserve current operation. If those obligations accumulate faster than flexibility, liquidity, and resilience capacity, the system becomes more disruption-sensitive over time even while outwardly appearing financially functional.

This sensitivity often expresses itself gradually.

Liquidity rebuilding slows first.

Margins become thinner.

Timing coordination requires more attention.

Recovery after disruption takes longer.

Future obligations consume larger portions of income before new flexibility can develop.

The household adapts incrementally to increasing operational pressure because the structure still functions during stable periods.

But functioning and resilience are not identical conditions.

A household can remain operational while gradually becoming more fragile underneath.

This is one reason visible income or visible consumption alone cannot fully explain financial stability.

Operational resilience depends on how much flexibility remains after recurring obligations are paid, how quickly liquidity can recover after disruption, and how much instability the structure can absorb before pressure spreads.

Baseline inflation directly affects all of these conditions because elevated operating thresholds reduce the system's remaining adaptability.

The household therefore becomes increasingly dependent on continuity.

Stable income timing matters more.

Irregular expenses become more disruptive.

Liquidity shocks create larger effects.

Recovery periods extend longer.

Future obligations leave less room for adjustment.

Over time, the structure may still appear stable externally while carrying rising instability internally.

This chapter reframes lifestyle-related debt away from simplistic behavioral judgments.

The issue is not merely spending more.

The issue is that financed obligation layering gradually changes the household's baseline operating structure until ordinary continuity itself becomes more expensive to maintain.

And because this process usually develops slowly, many households do not fully recognize how much obligation density has accumulated until the entire structure is examined clearly.

That broader visibility becomes increasingly important before instability accelerates further.

Seeing the Full Debt System

Many households experience debt as fragmented pressure.

A credit card balance exists in one account. An auto loan operates through another institution. Student loan payments arrive on separate schedules. A financing plan drafts automatically twice each month. Medical balances exist in a different portal entirely. Buy-now-pay-later obligations continue operating quietly in the background. Several subscriptions renew automatically across multiple payment methods. Minimum payments cluster around certain weeks while income arrives on different timing patterns.

The household feels pressure continuously.

But the structure producing that pressure often remains only partially visible at any one moment.

This fragmentation matters because systems are harder to stabilize when they cannot be seen clearly.

Most financially strained households do not operate under a single isolated debt obligation. They operate inside overlapping structures:
multiple balances,
multiple due dates,
multiple payment systems,
multiple timing demands,
and multiple recurring claims against future income operating simultaneously.

Yet these obligations are often experienced separately rather than collectively.

One balance receives attention today.

Another becomes visible when a payment alert arrives.

A third appears during a statement cycle.

An auto draft processes in the background without much ongoing visibility.

The household responds to pieces of the structure without fully seeing the structure itself.

This creates structural blind spots.

That invisibility increases instability.

When obligations remain fragmented, coordination weakens. Timing congestion becomes harder to identify. Liquidity pressure spreads quietly. Overlapping obligations become difficult to evaluate collectively. Risk points remain hidden until disruption exposes them directly.

This is why visibility itself becomes a stabilizing mechanism.

Debt Mapping is the process of organizing balances, rates, minimum payments, due dates, payment structures, risk points, recurring obligations, and liquidity pressures into one visible operational system.

The important word here is "system."

Debt mapping is not simply creating a list of balances. It is understanding how obligations interact across the household structure as one interconnected operating environment.

This changes the way pressure is interpreted.

When debt remains fragmented, the household often experiences instability emotionally before understanding it structurally. Pressure feels constant but difficult to locate precisely. Financial strain appears everywhere at once without a clear operational explanation for why flexibility keeps disappearing so quickly.

A household may know approximate balances individually while still lacking visibility into:

the total recurring obligation load,
the density of due dates,
the concentration of minimum payments,
the amount of income already committed before the month begins,
the interaction between repayment timing and income timing,
or the cumulative effect of overlapping obligations operating simultaneously.

But visibility changes coordination capacity.

Once obligations become visible together, pressure sources become easier to identify. Timing conflicts become clearer. Risk concentration becomes more obvious. The relationship between obligations and liquidity becomes easier to understand. Areas of recurring instability stop feeling random because the interaction pattern becomes visible.

Clarity reduces ambiguity.

Ambiguity amplifies pressure.

A household operating inside fragmented visibility often spends substantial energy reacting to obligations individually rather than understanding the structure collectively. One bill feels urgent this week. Another balance becomes stressful next week. A delayed payment creates pressure in one area while quietly weakening liquidity elsewhere.

Without full visibility, the household experiences recurring pressure without seeing how the pieces reinforce one another operationally.

This is why mapping becomes stabilizing even before repayment behavior changes materially.

The system becomes interpretable.

A complete debt map usually includes several interconnected categories operating together.

Balances matter because they reveal the size of active obligations.

Interest rates matter because they influence accumulation drag and repayment persistence.

Minimum payments matter because they determine recurring obligation load against future income.

Due dates matter because timing congestion affects coordination pressure and flow stability.

Recurring drafts matter because automatic obligations continue operating even when attention shifts elsewhere.

Income timing matters because repayment schedules interact directly with cash flow sequencing.

Liquidity reserves matter because they determine shock absorption capacity and timing flexibility.

Variable obligations matter because some costs fluctuate unpredictably across periods.

Risk exposure points matter because certain obligations or timing structures create disproportionate instability if disruption occurs.

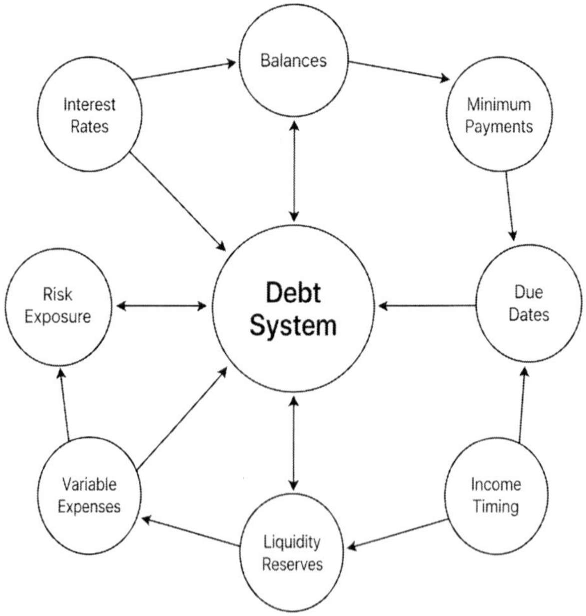

[Figure 6: The Debt Stability Map]

Once these elements become visible together, the interconnected nature of debt becomes much easier to understand.

Debt obligations do not operate independently.

A higher minimum payment in one area reduces available liquidity elsewhere.

A timing mismatch between income and one obligation may increase revolving pressure across several balances simultaneously.

An elevated housing payment may narrow flexibility enough that irregular costs increasingly move toward substitution debt.

A repayment structure absorbing too much cash flow may slow reserve rebuilding and increase future shock sensitivity.

Each obligation affects the entire operating environment around it.

This is one reason isolated account thinking often misses structural instability.

A household may focus intensely on one visible balance while overlooking the cumulative effect of obligation density elsewhere. One account may feel emotionally stressful while another quietly creates greater operational compression through timing congestion or recurring minimum pressure.

The issue is rarely one balance alone.

The issue is how balances interact together inside the broader structure.

This is also why some households feel persistent financial pressure even when no single obligation appears individually catastrophic.

The pressure is cumulative.

Several moderate obligations operating simultaneously may compress flexibility more aggressively than one large visible balance. Multiple recurring drafts, overlapping due dates, revolving balances, financing plans, and automatic payments collectively create operational density even if each individual obligation appears manageable in isolation.

Debt mapping makes this cumulative pressure visible.

Many households underestimate total obligation density until everything is viewed together simultaneously.

One financing plan here.

Several recurring services there.

Multiple revolving balances remaining active quietly.

Auto drafts operating continuously in the background.

Timing conflicts spreading across income periods.

Minimum payments consuming more future cash flow than expected.

Individually manageable.

Collectively compressive.

This cumulative visibility often changes how the household understands its own condition.

Importantly, visibility can initially feel emotionally uncomfortable because fragmented awareness sometimes functions as temporary pressure reduction. Looking at one account at a time may feel easier than confronting the full structure together.

Partial visibility narrows emotional exposure temporarily.

But operationally, avoidance increases instability because unseen pressure points continue functioning whether they are acknowledged or not.

Visibility does not create instability.

Visibility reveals instability that already exists.

This distinction matters because households sometimes confuse discomfort with danger. Seeing the full structure clearly may initially feel heavier simply because the obligation density becomes fully visible for the first time. But the obligations were already operating beforehand. Mapping removes fragmentation from the interpretation process.

This makes debt mapping fundamentally different from shame-based financial confrontation.

The goal is not emotional intensity.

The goal is operational clarity.

A household cannot coordinate timing conflicts effectively if timing conflicts remain only partially visible. Liquidity cannot be protected properly if recurring obligation density is underestimated. Shock exposure cannot be reduced if the structure's pressure concentrations remain hidden across disconnected accounts.

Visibility improves decision quality because the household stops reacting purely to whichever obligation feels most emotionally immediate.

Without mapping, financial decisions often become reactive. The loudest bill receives attention first. The most stressful balance dominates attention. Short-term urgency overrides structural interpretation because no integrated operational view exists.

Once the structure becomes visible together, decision-making changes.

Recurring pressure concentrations become easier to identify.

Timing congestion becomes clearer.

High-friction balances become more obvious.

Liquidity weaknesses become measurable rather than vaguely stressful.

Obligation layering becomes easier to interpret collectively.

The household can begin evaluating the structure systemically instead of emotionally.

This does not automatically solve instability.

But stabilization becomes much harder without accurate visibility.

You cannot coordinate what you cannot fully see.

This chapter also connects directly to the earlier mechanisms in the book because debt mapping makes those mechanisms operationally visible.

Obligation load becomes measurable when all recurring payments are viewed together instead of separately.

Runway compression becomes visible when the relationship between obligations, liquidity, and available recovery time is mapped clearly.

Payment tolerance limits become easier to identify once recurring fixed obligations are compared against income variability and available flexibility.

Accumulation drag concentrations emerge when balances, repayment structures, and interest persistence are visible simultaneously.

Flow misalignment becomes easier to recognize once income timing and due-date density are viewed together.

Shock exposure points become clearer when weak liquidity and elevated recurring obligations are mapped across the same structure.

Baseline inflation becomes easier to recognize once recurring operating costs are viewed collectively instead of individually.

Each mechanism becomes more interpretable through visibility.

This is why debt mapping is not merely informational organization.

It is structural clarification.

The household moves from fragmented reaction toward integrated interpretation.

And often, this alone changes the emotional character of financial pressure significantly.

Diffuse pressure tends to feel heavier because the source remains unclear. When obligations remain scattered and partially visible, instability can feel constant yet difficult to define precisely. The household senses compression without fully understanding where the compression originates.

Clarity reduces some of that ambiguity.

Not because the obligations disappear, but because the structure becomes understandable.

The household can finally see:

where the pressure concentrates,
where timing conflicts occur,
where liquidity remains weakest,
where recurring obligations cluster,
where repayment drag persists,
and where flexibility continues narrowing.

This visibility creates the foundation for meaningful stabilization later.

Because once the structure becomes visible, obligations can finally be evaluated according to their actual operational impact rather than their emotional visibility alone.

And that naturally leads to the next stage of debt stability:
understanding which obligations create the greatest operational pressure inside the system.

Prioritizing Debt Without Panic

Most households experience debt as undifferentiated pressure.

Balances exist across multiple accounts. Notifications arrive continuously. Minimum payments overlap. Due dates cluster together. Interest accumulates quietly in the background. Auto drafts process automatically while new expenses continue appearing. Timing stress spreads across the month without clear boundaries between one obligation and another.

Everything appears urgent at once.

A credit card balance demands attention. A vehicle payment approaches. A financing plan drafts unexpectedly. A medical payment remains unresolved. Several smaller obligations continue operating quietly beneath the surface while larger balances dominate emotional attention.

This kind of environment naturally produces reactive prioritization.

The household responds to whichever obligation feels most immediate in the moment. A collection notice creates urgency. A missed call from a creditor pulls attention toward one balance. A smaller account feels psychologically irritating and becomes the focus. An older debt carries emotional weight because it has remained unresolved for years. A particular balance creates embarrassment, frustration, or exhaustion and therefore absorbs disproportionate attention.

But emotional visibility and operational pressure are not always the same thing.

An obligation that feels emotionally intense may not necessarily create the greatest structural instability. At the same time, an obligation receiving little emotional attention may quietly compress liquidity, distort timing coordination, or weaken flexibility far more aggressively than the balance dominating immediate focus.

This distinction matters because stabilization depends on understanding pressure structurally rather than only emotionally.

Pressure Ranking is the process of prioritizing obligations according to their operational impact on liquidity, timing stability, recurring strain, risk exposure, and system flexibility rather than emotional intensity alone.

The purpose of pressure ranking is not optimization for its own sake.

It is clarification.

Once obligations are interpreted according to how they actually affect system stability, diffuse pressure begins separating into understandable categories. The structure stops feeling like one undifferentiated mass of financial stress and becomes more operationally visible.

This changes coordination.

A household no longer reacts only to whichever balance feels loudest emotionally. Instead, obligations begin revealing different kinds of pressure operating simultaneously across the structure.

Not all debt creates equal instability.

Some obligations create pressure primarily because of recurring payment size. A large monthly obligation may continuously absorb liquidity and narrow flexibility even if the balance itself is not emotionally dominant.

Some obligations destabilize timing. Due dates cluster aggressively around income gaps. Automatic drafts create sequencing pressure. Timing mismatches increase the likelihood of revolving substitution behavior even when total income remains technically sufficient.

Some obligations create persistence through repayment structure. High-interest revolving balances may remain active for long periods, continuously generating accumulation drag while slowing liquidity rebuilding across the broader system.

Other obligations threaten continuity directly. A vehicle loan tied to transportation reliability, housing-related obligations, or obligations connected to essential operational infrastructure may create disproportionate instability if disruption occurs.

Some balances create escalation risk because penalties, fees, or repayment structures intensify rapidly after missed payments. Others repeatedly trigger substitution pressure because they interact poorly with variable income timing or irregular expenses.

The important point is that debt pressure is multidimensional.

One obligation may create liquidity compression.

Another may create timing instability.

Another may create emotional exhaustion.

Another may generate long-term accumulation drag.

Another may threaten continuity if disrupted unexpectedly.

The issue is not determining which debt appears morally worse.

The issue is identifying which obligations compress the household structure most aggressively.

A smaller balance with severe timing pressure may destabilize the system more than a larger obligation operating on a manageable structure. A moderate recurring payment tied to essential transportation may create greater continuity risk than a larger but more stable long-term obligation. Several small recurring drafts may collectively weaken liquidity more aggressively than one visible major balance.

Without structural interpretation, these differences remain difficult to recognize.

Everything simply feels stressful.

This is one reason fragmented debt often creates such intense psychological pressure. The household senses compression everywhere at once but lacks a clear operational framework for interpreting where instability actually concentrates most heavily.

Pressure ranking reduces that ambiguity.

Importantly, emotional pressure still matters.

An obligation generating constant psychological strain can affect operational stability directly. Continuous stress surrounding a particular balance may dominate attention, weaken coordination quality, increase avoidance behavior, or narrow decision clarity. A household repeatedly overwhelmed by one obligation may begin reacting impulsively elsewhere in the structure simply because cognitive and emotional capacity are already heavily consumed.

Psychological load therefore remains part of the system.

But it is one variable inside the larger structure rather than the sole organizing principle.

This distinction matters because emotionally driven prioritization sometimes creates operational distortion. A household may focus intensely on eliminating one emotionally uncomfortable balance while leaving more destabilizing obligations structurally untouched elsewhere. The emotional relief may feel temporarily meaningful while timing instability, liquidity compression, or recurring strain continues operating beneath the surface.

Operational pressure and emotional pressure overlap sometimes, but not always.

Structural interpretation helps separate the two clearly enough for more coherent coordination to emerge.

This becomes especially important during periods of panic.

When all obligations feel equally urgent, decision quality often compresses rapidly. The household moves from interpretation into reaction. Liquidity gets redirected inconsistently. Timing coordination weakens. One payment is prioritized emotionally while another destabilizing obligation receives less attention than its structural impact warrants. Reactive substitutions increase because pressure is no longer being interpreted clearly across the entire system.

Diffuse pressure fragments attention.

And fragmented attention tends to increase instability.

A household reacting continuously to immediate urgency often loses visibility into the larger operational structure. Short-term emotional intensity overrides broader coordination logic. Obligations are managed individually rather than systemically. Pressure spreads faster because the structure is no longer being interpreted coherently.

This is one reason panic tends to amplify instability even when the underlying financial structure itself has not changed materially.

Panic compresses interpretation capacity.

When everything feels urgent simultaneously, the household often begins operating tactically without maintaining structural visibility. Decisions become shorter in time horizon. Liquidity may move toward immediate relief instead of broader stabilization. Timing errors increase because coordination bandwidth narrows under pressure.

Pressure ranking reduces some of this fragmentation.

Once obligations are evaluated structurally, pressure begins organizing itself into understandable categories. High-risk pressure points become clearer. Timing bottlenecks become visible. Obligations threatening continuity stand apart from obligations generating primarily emotional discomfort. Recurring strain concentrations become easier to identify. Areas where liquidity weakens most aggressively become more visible.

The household may still experience pressure, but it becomes more interpretable.

And interpretability itself is stabilizing.

Clarity improves coordination.

This does not mean the household suddenly becomes free from financial strain. Prioritization alone does not eliminate obligation load, restore liquidity instantly, or reverse accumulation drag immediately.

But reduced ambiguity improves operational capacity.

A household that understands where pressure concentrates usually coordinates more effectively than a household reacting emotionally to fragmented obligations without structural interpretation.

This chapter therefore represents an important transition in the broader debt system framework.

Earlier chapters explained how instability forms.

Obligation load established how debt creates recurring claims against future income.

Runway compression explained how obligations reduce operational time under disruption.

Payment tolerance showed why some structures remain absorbable while others destabilize under relatively ordinary strain.

Accumulation drag explained why repayment pressure often persists much longer than households expect.

Flow misalignment demonstrated how timing instability amplifies recurring pressure.

Substitution pressure showed how ordinary shortfalls gradually become borrowed capacity.

Shock conversion explained how liquidity failure transforms temporary disruption into long-term obligations.

Baseline inflation revealed how financed lifestyle expansion quietly raises operating thresholds over time.

Debt mapping then made the structure visible as one interconnected operating environment.

Pressure ranking becomes possible only after that visibility exists.

Debt mapping revealed the structure.

Pressure ranking interprets the structure.

This distinction matters because visibility alone does not automatically produce coordination. A household may see the full system clearly while still feeling overwhelmed if every obligation appears equally important simultaneously.

Interpretation organizes visibility into structure.

The structure begins separating into different forms of pressure:
liquidity compression,
timing congestion,
shock sensitivity,
accumulation persistence,
continuity exposure,
and recurring strain concentration.

Once these distinctions become visible, prioritization becomes calmer and more coherent.

Because the structure stops behaving like undifferentiated chaos.

This also changes the relationship between urgency and stability.

Many households interpret the loudest pressure as the most dangerous pressure. But operational instability does not always announce itself emotionally. Some obligations quietly weaken flexibility month after month without creating immediate emotional intensity. Others generate substantial anxiety while creating less actual system compression than the household perceives.

Pressure ranking helps separate visibility from impact.

The household can begin asking different questions:
Which obligations reduce liquidity most aggressively?
Which obligations destabilize timing coordination?
Which obligations increase substitution risk?
Which obligations threaten continuity if disrupted?
Which obligations extend accumulation drag most severely?
Which obligations compress runway most rapidly?

These questions shift attention away from emotional reaction and toward structural interpretation.

Again, this is not optimization culture.

The goal is not creating the "perfect" repayment sequence or engineering an idealized financial structure through constant tactical adjustment.

The goal is reducing instability through clearer understanding.

A household operating with structural clarity generally makes more coherent decisions than a household operating under diffuse panic.

This becomes especially important because instability often amplifies when obligations remain emotionally undifferentiated. If every balance feels equally threatening, the nervous system responds as though the entire structure is collapsing simultaneously even when actual operational risk remains concentrated in more specific areas.

Pressure ranking narrows the field.

The household can finally see where flexibility is weakening most aggressively, where timing coordination matters most, where liquidity exposure remains highest, and where recurring obligations create the greatest strain relative to available capacity.

It improves sequencing quality.

It reduces fragmented attention.

And it creates space for more deliberate stabilization across time.

Importantly, this process should not be confused with perfection.

No household interprets complex financial structures flawlessly. Conditions change. Income shifts. Expenses evolve. Obligations interact differently during periods of instability than during stable periods. Pressure ranking itself may change as the structure changes.

But even imperfect visibility and prioritization usually improve coordination compared to fragmented emotional reaction alone.

Because stabilization begins with understanding pressure accurately.

And accurate interpretation creates calmer decision environments than diffuse urgency.

The household now possesses something earlier chapters intentionally delayed:

not simply awareness that pressure exists,
but visibility into how pressure behaves across the structure itself.

That changes the nature of financial coordination fundamentally.

The system no longer appears as scattered balances competing randomly for attention.

It begins behaving like an interconnected structure that can be interpreted, stabilized, and gradually reorganized with greater clarity over time.

And once pressure becomes interpretable, rebuilding flexibility becomes far more possible than it first appeared when everything felt urgent simultaneously.

Minimum Payments and False Stability

Minimum payments often create a feeling of temporary order.

The required amount is paid. Accounts remain current. Statements continue showing compliance. Penalties are avoided. Collection activity stays limited or absent. Access to credit may remain available. The household continues functioning without obvious external breakdown.

From the outside, the structure can appear stable.

Payments are still being made.

No visible crisis has occurred.

This creates an understandable sense of relief. A household under financial pressure often experiences immediate anxiety reduction when obligations remain current because current status signals continuity. The system appears operational. The accounts remain active. The immediate threat of disruption feels contained.

But current status and structural improvement are not the same condition.

A household may maintain payment continuity while experiencing very little actual recovery in flexibility, liquidity, or long-term stability.

This distinction becomes especially important when minimum payments remain active across multiple balances for extended periods.

The mechanism operating underneath this condition is the Maintenance Trap.

Maintenance Trap is the condition where minimum payments keep accounts current while preventing actual control from improving because balances remain active, interest continues, obligations persist, and flexibility does not recover meaningfully.

The important point is that minimum payments are not inherently irresponsible or harmful.

In many periods, minimum payments may preserve continuity during instability. A household facing temporary pressure may need to maintain accounts conservatively while protecting liquidity, stabilizing income timing, or absorbing disruption elsewhere in the system. Minimum payments can reduce immediate escalation risk. They can help preserve operational continuity while conditions remain unstable.

The problem emerges when payment compliance is mistaken for structural recovery.

Making the required payment and improving the system are not automatically the same thing.

Current means the required payment was made.

Control means the household's flexibility, liquidity position, obligation load, and recovery capacity are improving across time.

A household can remain fully current while still operating inside a structurally compressed system.

This distinction often becomes difficult to recognize because minimum payments preserve visible order. Statements continue arriving normally. Accounts remain open. Payment history remains intact. Immediate penalties remain limited. The structure appears functional enough to avoid obvious failure.

But underneath that continuity, the system may remain almost unchanged operationally.

Balances may decline slowly.

Interest may continue absorbing substantial portions of repayment flow.

Recurring obligations may remain active month after month.

Liquidity rebuilding may remain weak.

Runway may remain compressed.

The household may still depend heavily on uninterrupted income continuity simply to maintain ordinary operation.

In these situations, payments are preserving the structure more than changing the structure.

Minimum payments often function this way because they are designed primarily to maintain account continuity rather than accelerate flexibility recovery. The account remains active. The repayment structure continues functioning. The obligation remains operationally alive across long periods of time.

This becomes especially visible with revolving balances.

A household may make payments consistently every month while principal reduction remains relatively slow because portions of repayment flow continue moving toward interest, fees, or carrying costs instead of materially reducing the underlying obligation.

The household experiences steady outflow without equally steady pressure reduction.

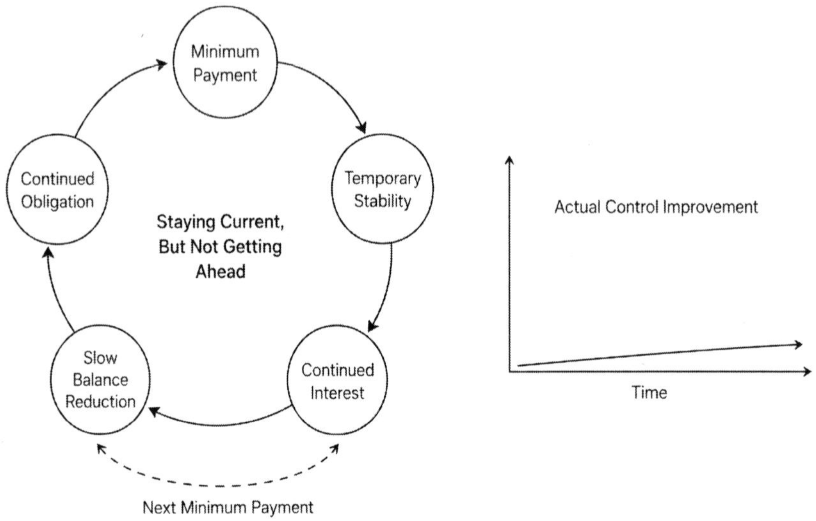

[Figure 7: The Minimum Payment Maintenance Trap]

This creates a form of false stability.

The system appears stable because nothing visibly collapses.

Accounts remain current.

Payments continue processing.

Statements show compliance.

No immediate crisis forces rapid correction.

But the underlying operating condition may remain largely unchanged.

The household may still possess very little margin after recurring obligations are paid. Liquidity may remain thin. Runway may remain short. Small disruptions may still create substitution pressure. Timing mismatches may still destabilize coordination quickly. The balances themselves may remain active for long periods despite continuous payment activity.

This is not necessarily stabilization.

Often it is maintenance.

The distinction matters because maintenance mode can persist for years without producing meaningful improvement in household flexibility.

A household operating inside the maintenance trap may feel constant movement without substantial recovery. Payments leave the account every month. Effort continues. Financial attention remains active. Yet the structure itself changes very slowly.

The obligations persist.

The pressure persists.

The narrow operating range persists.

This interaction connects directly to accumulation drag.

Earlier chapters explained that accumulation drag extends instability timelines because repayment systems often reduce principal slowly while interest and carrying costs remain active. Minimum payment structures can intensify this condition because repayment flow may continue circulating through the system without significantly reducing obligation load quickly enough to restore flexibility meaningfully.

The household keeps paying.

But the balances remain alive.

This is one reason many households feel financially exhausted despite remaining technically compliant for long periods. The effort required to maintain continuity remains high while visible structural improvement appears limited.

Again, this should not be interpreted morally.

The issue is not laziness, irresponsibility, or lack of discipline. Many households making minimum payments are operating under legitimate structural constraints:

thin liquidity,
compressed runway,
income variability,
elevated operating costs,
or repeated disruption exposure.

In some periods, maintaining continuity conservatively may be entirely reasonable.

The important issue is interpretation.

Minimum payments preserve continuity.

But continuity and recovery are not identical conditions.

A household may avoid visible failure while still remaining deeply vulnerable to ordinary instability.

This vulnerability often becomes hidden because payment compliance creates psychological relief. The accounts remain functional. Immediate pressure eases temporarily. The absence of visible escalation can create the impression that meaningful stabilization is occurring.

That emotional relief matters operationally. Reduced panic can improve coordination quality. Preserving continuity may prevent additional disruption during unstable periods.

But if the structure itself does not gradually improve, the household may remain trapped in long-term maintenance mode while believing it is steadily recovering.

This is where false stability becomes dangerous.

False stability delays structural recognition.

If the household interprets minimum payment compliance as sufficient evidence of improvement, deeper instability may remain largely unexamined. Liquidity may still fail to rebuild meaningfully. Recurring obligations may still absorb too much future income. Timing pressure may remain persistent. Accumulation drag may continue extending repayment duration quietly in the background.

The system continues functioning, but flexibility does not return.

This distinction becomes clearer once minimum payments are evaluated through the broader debt map rather than through isolated account status alone.

A minimum payment on one balance may create relatively little operational instability if the household is simultaneously protecting liquidity, stabilizing timing coordination, or preventing escalation elsewhere. In some situations, maintaining conservative repayment structures temporarily may improve overall stability by preserving flexibility during uncertain periods.

But when multiple balances are all being maintained only at minimum levels while liquidity remains weak and recurring obligations stay active across long periods, the structure may no longer be progressing meaningfully toward greater resilience.

The system is being preserved rather than improved.

This is why minimum payments should be interpreted through pressure ranking rather than through current status alone.

An account remaining current does not necessarily mean the pressure attached to it has become manageable. The more important question is how that obligation affects overall system stability.

Does the obligation continue compressing liquidity aggressively?

Does it extend runway compression?

Does it maintain recurring timing pressure?

Does it increase substitution sensitivity?

Does it continue generating accumulation drag across long repayment periods?

Does the structure around the obligation show signs of increasing flexibility, or only continued maintenance?

These questions matter more than current status by itself.

Because current status measures compliance.

Stability measures recovery capacity.

The distinction between those two conditions becomes increasingly important as debt systems mature across time. A household may spend years successfully maintaining obligations while remaining structurally fragile underneath because maintenance activity alone does not guarantee flexibility recovery.

This is especially true when recurring obligations continue absorbing nearly all available monthly margin.

If most available cash flow continues moving toward maintaining existing obligations, the household may struggle to rebuild reserves, restore adaptability, or meaningfully expand runway. The structure survives month to month but remains highly dependent on continuity because too little flexibility exists underneath the payment structure itself.

In this environment, even small disruptions can still create outsized effects.

A temporary income reduction may destabilize timing coordination quickly.

An irregular expense may trigger new substitution pressure.

A repair or medical event may interrupt repayment flow.

Liquidity rebuilding may reverse rapidly because reserves remained thin throughout the maintenance period.

The household therefore remains operationally vulnerable despite long periods of technical compliance.

Again, none of this means minimum payments are automatically wrong.

The issue is not the existence of minimum payments.

The issue is whether the structure surrounding those payments is actually improving.

Is liquidity recovering gradually?

Is obligation load declining meaningfully?

Is runway expanding?

Is flexibility increasing?

Are balances shrinking in ways that materially improve future operating capacity?

Is the household becoming less disruption-sensitive over time?

These are structural questions rather than emotional ones.

Because repayment only improves stability when it improves the household's ability to absorb future conditions more effectively than before.

This chapter therefore reframes minimum payment behavior away from simplistic financial morality.

The issue is not whether a household "should" always pay aggressively or eliminate balances rapidly regardless of conditions. In some environments, preserving continuity conservatively may protect the system from greater instability elsewhere.

But current status alone should never be confused with restored control.

A household may remain current while operating inside narrow margins for years if repayment activity preserves obligations faster than it restores flexibility.

That is the maintenance trap.

And recognizing the difference between maintenance and recovery changes how repayment progress must be interpreted across the entire debt structure.

Because durable repayment depends not only on willingness to pay, but on whether the underlying cash flow structure can support real pressure reduction without creating new instability elsewhere in the system.

Cash Flow Before Aggression

Many households eventually reach a point where debt pressure becomes impossible to ignore comfortably.

The balances remain active. Minimum payments continue cycling through the system. Liquidity rebuilding feels slow or inconsistent. Timing pressure persists month after month. A growing awareness develops that the structure cannot remain permanently suspended between maintenance and recovery without eventually requiring deeper adjustment.

At that point, a common assumption emerges.

If debt is creating pressure, then more aggressive repayment should create faster stability.

The logic appears straightforward. Larger payments reduce balances faster. Faster reduction should shorten repayment timelines. Shorter timelines should improve flexibility more quickly. Intense repayment effort therefore appears responsible, corrective, and structurally efficient.

For many households, aggressive repayment also carries emotional meaning.

Periods of debt pressure often generate frustration, embarrassment, fatigue, or anxiety. Once the household becomes serious about improving conditions, there can be a strong impulse toward immediate correction. Large payments feel productive. Aggressive reduction feels decisive. Faster repayment appears morally and emotionally aligned with regaining control.

But repayment itself operates inside the household system.

And that means repayment can become destabilizing if it absorbs too much operating capacity during the process.

This is the mechanism that matters in this chapter.

Repayment Capacity is the amount of debt reduction a household can sustain while preserving liquidity, operational continuity, flexibility, and shock absorption.

The important distinction is that repayment capacity is not determined only by theoretical affordability.

A household may technically possess enough income to pay larger amounts toward debt temporarily. But if those payments eliminate remaining liquidity, compress timing flexibility, weaken shock absorption, or destabilize ordinary operation, the repayment structure itself may become fragile.

The issue is not unwillingness to repay.

The issue is whether repayment intensity fits inside real household conditions without undermining the system's ability to continue functioning reliably.

Every repayment dollar comes from current operating capacity.

That seems obvious initially, but the implications become more important once the broader structure is examined carefully.

Repayment competes against liquidity rebuilding.

Repayment competes against reserve restoration.

Repayment competes against timing flexibility.

Repayment competes against future shock absorption.

Repayment competes against operational margin.

This creates tension inside the system because households under pressure often feel emotionally driven toward aggressive reduction precisely when the structure itself may already be operating with narrow tolerance ranges.

A household emerging from prolonged financial strain may begin directing nearly all remaining surplus toward balances after becoming determined to improve conditions quickly. Savings rebuilding slows or stops entirely. Liquidity remains thin because available cash flow is redirected aggressively toward repayment. Timing flexibility narrows because little reserve capacity remains underneath ordinary operation.

Initially, this may feel productive.

Balances begin shrinking faster.

The household experiences movement instead of maintenance.

The emotional contrast between prior stagnation and visible reduction can feel significant.

But if repayment intensity removes too much remaining operating margin, the structure may become increasingly vulnerable during the repayment process itself.

An irregular expense appears.

A repair interrupts sequencing.

Income timing shifts temporarily.

Work hours fluctuate.

A medical cost arrives unexpectedly.

Liquidity proves too thin to absorb the disruption cleanly.

Substitution pressure reappears.

Balances expand again.

The repayment structure destabilizes.

This cycle is extremely common, and it is often interpreted incorrectly.

Many households interpret repayment failure as evidence of weak discipline, inconsistency, or insufficient commitment. But frequently the issue is structural rather than motivational.

The repayment structure itself lacked sufficient tolerance for ordinary instability.

A repayment plan that cannot survive normal disruption is not operationally stable.

This distinction matters because many aggressive repayment approaches quietly assume uninterrupted conditions. The repayment schedule is built as though income timing will remain predictable, expenses will remain stable, emergencies will remain absent, and household operation will proceed without meaningful irregularity across long periods of time.

Real household systems do not behave that way.

Repairs occur.

Expenses cluster unevenly.

Income fluctuates.

Timing mismatches appear.

Medical costs emerge.

Seasonal shifts affect cash flow.

Ordinary instability remains normal even inside improving financial structures.

If repayment intensity leaves no room for that instability, the system becomes brittle.

The household may reduce balances temporarily while simultaneously weakening resilience underneath the repayment structure itself.

This creates an important distinction between visible progress and stable progress.

Visible progress focuses on balance reduction speed.

Stable progress focuses on whether the household's overall operating condition is improving while repayment occurs.

These are not always the same thing.

A household aggressively directing every available dollar toward balances may reduce debt faster temporarily while remaining highly disruption-sensitive because liquidity never rebuilds meaningfully. Another household repaying more gradually while preserving reserves and flexibility may appear slower externally while improving structural resilience more effectively over time.

The difference becomes especially visible after disruption occurs.

The aggressively compressed structure may reverse quickly because no absorption capacity remained underneath the repayment plan. The more balanced structure may continue progressing despite instability because liquidity and operating margin preserved coordination capacity during disruption.

This is why liquidity often matters more than temporary repayment acceleration during long repayment periods.

Liquidity protects continuity.

It protects timing coordination.

It absorbs irregularity.

It creates adaptation capacity between obligations and instability.

Without liquidity, repayment systems become interruption-sensitive. One disruption may reverse months of progress because the structure relied too heavily on uninterrupted conditions remaining perfectly stable.

This creates emotional fatigue as well.

A household repeatedly attempting highly aggressive repayment structures may experience recurring cycles of compression and reversal. Intense repayment begins. Margin narrows sharply. A disruption interrupts progress. Balances re-expand. Frustration increases. Repayment effort pauses temporarily. Then another aggressive cycle begins later under worse structural conditions.

Over time, this pattern often weakens operational confidence because repayment begins feeling unstable rather than sustainable.

Again, the issue is not lack of effort.

Often the issue is that repayment intensity exceeded actual repayment capacity.

This distinction changes how repayment itself must be interpreted.

Emotionally reactive repayment often emerges after fear, panic, shame, or exhaustion. The household wants visible correction quickly because debt pressure has become psychologically heavy. Aggressive reduction appears emotionally cleansing. Maximum intensity feels responsible.

But emotionally reactive repayment frequently compresses present operating margin too aggressively because it assumes current intensity can continue indefinitely regardless of future instability.

Sustainable repayment behaves differently.

Sustainable repayment preserves continuity.

It leaves room for irregularity.

It protects liquidity gradually.

It recognizes variability inside ordinary household operation.

It improves flexibility over time instead of sacrificing flexibility temporarily for faster visible reduction.

Importantly, sustainable repayment may appear slower externally while strengthening the structure more effectively internally.

This is difficult sometimes because modern financial culture often treats repayment speed as the primary measure of responsibility or seriousness. Faster elimination appears emotionally impressive. Aggressive reduction appears disciplined.

But operationally, repayment exists inside cash flow systems rather than inside abstract payoff calculations.

Monthly income timing matters.

Obligation density matters.

Existing liquidity matters.

Recurring operating costs matter.

Shock exposure matters.

Income variability matters.

Theoretical repayment ability and operational repayment ability are not identical.

A household may technically possess enough income to increase repayment substantially, but only by eliminating nearly all remaining flexibility in the process.

That creates instability risk.

This becomes especially important once prior mechanisms from earlier chapters are considered together.

Runway compression means the household already possesses limited operating time under disruption.

Flow misalignment means income timing may remain imperfect.

Accumulation drag means balances may continue interacting with interest and persistence across long periods.

Substitution pressure means ordinary shortfalls may still emerge operationally.

Shock conversion means future disruptions may become debt if liquidity remains insufficient.

Baseline inflation means recurring operating thresholds may already be elevated.

Maintenance trap dynamics may still keep balances active despite continuous payments.

Under these conditions, repayment intensity that ignores liquidity and operating margin can destabilize the structure even while balances are declining temporarily.

This is why repayment capacity must be interpreted structurally rather than emotionally.

A stable repayment structure usually shows certain broader operating improvements gradually emerging alongside balance reduction.

Liquidity slowly begins rebuilding instead of remaining permanently exhausted.

Timing pressure decreases modestly.

Substitution behavior becomes less frequent.

Recurring obligations begin shrinking without destroying remaining flexibility.

Recovery after disruption improves gradually instead of collapsing repayment momentum entirely.

The household becomes less dependent on perfect continuity because more operating tolerance exists underneath the repayment structure itself.

Operational calm increases slowly because the structure no longer requires constant defensive coordination simply to remain functional.

These shifts matter because repayment is not separate from household stability.

Repayment occurs inside the system.

The household must survive the repayment period itself.

That point is often underestimated.

Debt reduction can take years inside real household conditions. During those years, the structure continues operating. Income continues fluctuating. Repairs continue occurring. Timing mismatches continue appearing. Irregular expenses continue emerging. Life variability does not pause simply because repayment has become a priority.

A repayment structure that repeatedly collapses under ordinary instability is not sustainably reducing debt pressure even if periods of temporary progress occur along the way.

This does not mean repayment should become passive or indefinitely delayed. The issue is not avoiding repayment effort. The issue is whether repayment pressure coexists realistically with the household's need for continuity, resilience, and adaptability throughout the process.

Because a household that destroys all remaining operating margin during repayment may eventually recreate instability faster than balances decline.

This is why repayment capacity becomes more important than repayment intensity alone.

Capacity reflects the system's ability to continue functioning while debt reduction occurs.

Intensity reflects how much pressure is being directed toward balances immediately.

The two are related, but they are not interchangeable.

A structure with strong repayment capacity may reduce debt steadily across long periods because liquidity, flexibility, and operating continuity remain sufficiently preserved to survive disruption without repeated collapse cycles.

A structure operating beyond repayment capacity may produce bursts of rapid reduction followed by destabilization, substitution, or repayment reversal because no resilience exists underneath the repayment effort itself.

This distinction often changes the emotional experience of repayment as well.

A household operating inside sustainable repayment conditions frequently experiences less panic over time because the structure becomes more survivable. Timing pressure eases modestly. Liquidity begins existing again in usable form. Irregular expenses stop threatening immediate destabilization quite as severely. Coordination becomes less reactive.

The progress may appear slower numerically.

But the structure itself becomes more stable.

And stability matters because repayment is ultimately valuable not merely for reducing balances, but for restoring flexibility, adaptability, and operational resilience across the household system itself.

That restoration occurs gradually.

Not through maximum intensity sustained briefly, but through repayment structures capable of surviving ordinary life conditions repeatedly across time without collapsing into new instability cycles.

The household therefore does not improve simply because balances decline.

The household improves when debt reduction and structural resilience begin strengthening together instead of competing destructively against one another.

At that point, repayment stops functioning as a reactive emergency effort and begins operating more like long-term stabilization inside the broader financial structure.

Reducing New Debt Formation

Many households experience debt reduction as a pattern of temporary progress followed by re-expansion.

A balance declines for several months. The payments appear to be working. The household feels movement after a long period of strain. Then an irregular expense appears before liquidity has fully recovered. A repair becomes necessary. Income arrives later than expected. A medical bill creates new pressure. A timing gap emerges between obligations and cash flow. A shortfall appears during an already narrow month.

The balance that had been shrinking begins growing again.

Or another balance expands while the first one continues declining.

This creates the familiar feeling of never getting ahead. The household is not doing nothing. Payments are being made. Effort is being applied. Some obligations may be shrinking. Yet the overall structure does not feel meaningfully more stable because new debt continues forming underneath the repayment process.

This is one reason repayment alone often feels incomplete.

Debt reduction improves the structure only when the conditions creating new debt begin weakening at the same time. If repayment reduces old obligations while recurring instability creates new ones, the system may recycle pressure rather than resolve it.

Leakage Interruption is the process of identifying and interrupting the recurring conditions that continuously regenerate debt pressure across the household structure.

The issue is not perfection. No household eliminates all irregularity. Repairs still occur. Income timing still shifts. Costs still rise unevenly. Emergencies still appear. Ordinary household operation contains variation.

The question is whether recurring operational gaps continue feeding new borrowing faster than stability can rebuild.

Repayment reduces prior obligation load. But recurring shortfalls can create new obligation load simultaneously. A household may pay down one revolving balance while another expands because irregular expenses keep arriving without enough liquidity to absorb them. A financing plan may be reduced while a new replacement cost enters the structure. A credit card balance may decline for several months and then rise again after a vehicle repair or delayed paycheck.

In these situations, the household may be moving in two directions at once.

Old debt is being reduced.

New debt is being generated.

The visible repayment effort is real, but the structure underneath may still be producing instability. If new obligation formation continues too frequently, repayment progress becomes fragile because flexibility does not have enough time to rebuild before the next shortfall appears.

This is not primarily a behavioral failure.

Most recurring debt formation does not emerge from one dramatic decision. It often develops through operational leakage.

Operational leakage is the repeated loss of flexibility through irregular costs, timing mismatches, elevated baseline obligations, thin liquidity, substitution behavior, and small shortfalls that appear manageable individually but accumulate across time.

A repair here. A school cost there. A seasonal utility spike. A delayed reimbursement. A few weeks of reduced hours. A subscription that continues unnoticed. A higher insurance premium. A replacement purchase that could not wait. None of these events may be large enough to explain instability by themselves.

Together, they prevent recovery from becoming durable.

This is why leakage matters more than isolated spending events. A household can avoid major discretionary expansion and still experience repeated debt regeneration if ordinary operation produces more shortfalls than available flexibility can absorb.

The structure does not need one catastrophic break.

It can weaken through repeated small gaps.

This is also why repayment can feel frustrating even when the household is making meaningful effort. Progress may be occurring in one area while pressure is reforming elsewhere. A balance shrinks, but liquidity remains thin. Minimum payments continue, but irregular expenses keep moving toward borrowed capacity. The household makes additional payments, but the repayment intensity leaves too little margin for the next disruption.

Eventually, repayment becomes a loop.

Money flows toward old balances.

A shortfall appears.

Borrowing fills the gap.

A new balance forms.

Repayment begins again.

The household may remain active and attentive through the entire cycle, yet the system does not stabilize because the conditions creating new obligations remain in place.

This is the difference between reducing debt and interrupting debt formation.

Debt reduction addresses existing obligations.

Leakage interruption addresses the forces that keep creating new obligations.

Both matter. But without interruption, repayment can become a maintenance cycle rather than a lasting stabilization process.

The sources of ongoing debt formation are rarely singular. More often, several small pressures interact at once.

Thin liquidity is one of the most important. When reserves are weak, ordinary irregularity has fewer places to go. A repair, timing gap, or medical expense cannot be absorbed directly. The household must preserve continuity somehow, so borrowed capacity becomes the temporary stabilizer. The expense passes, but the obligation remains.

Unstable income timing can create the same effect. A household may earn enough across a month or year while still experiencing short-term cash flow gaps because income and obligations do not align cleanly. When due dates arrive before inflow, revolving balances may bridge the gap. If this happens repeatedly, short-term timing support becomes recurring debt pressure.

Elevated recurring obligations also increase leakage. When baseline costs rise, less income remains available after fixed payments. The household may still function during ordinary periods, but irregular expenses become harder to absorb without substitution. The structure becomes more sensitive because the margin between normal operation and shortfall has narrowed.

Repayment structures themselves can create leakage if they exceed actual repayment capacity. Aggressive repayment may reduce balances temporarily while leaving too little operating margin underneath the plan. When ordinary instability appears, the household may need to borrow again simply because all available flexibility was already committed to repayment.

Delayed maintenance can also contribute. When liquidity is thin, households may postpone repairs or replacements to preserve short-term continuity. Sometimes delay is unavoidable. But postponed costs can return later in larger or more urgent form, increasing the likelihood that borrowed capacity becomes necessary when the expense finally arrives.

None of these sources functions as a single villain. The instability comes from interaction. Several modest pressures combine to create recurring shortfalls that repeatedly regenerate debt.

Liquidity interrupts this process because it absorbs instability before it converts into borrowing.

This is one of the clearest structural roles of reserves. Liquidity is not merely extra money sitting outside the system. It is interruption capacity.

A household with accessible reserves can encounter a repair without automatically creating a new balance. It can bridge a timing gap without relying immediately on revolving credit. It can absorb a temporary income delay without turning the delay into a repayment obligation. It can handle irregular expenses while preserving continuity.

Without liquidity, ordinary instability often defaults toward debt substitution automatically.

This does not mean liquidity prevents all pressure. A reserve may decline after absorbing disruption. Recovery may still take time. But the disruption remains more contained because it does not immediately become a recurring future claim against income.

That distinction is central to debt stability.

A household cannot reduce pressure sustainably if every irregular expense becomes a new obligation. Debt reduction improves stability only when future obligation growth slows at the same time. Otherwise, the structure remains trapped between repayment and regeneration.

This is why new debt formation must be understood as a structural signal.

If balances keep reforming, the question is not simply whether the household is committed enough to repayment. The more important question is what conditions keep producing shortfalls.

Is income timing unstable relative to due dates?

Are irregular expenses arriving without liquidity support?

Are recurring obligations leaving too little margin?

Is baseline operating cost too high relative to recovery capacity?

Is repayment intensity consuming the buffer needed to prevent reversal?

Are shortfalls seasonal, predictable, or connected to recurring timing patterns?

These are not questions of blame. They are questions of pattern recognition.

Households often underestimate how frequently shortfalls repeat because each event appears isolated in the moment. A repair feels separate from a delayed paycheck. A medical bill feels separate from a school expense. A seasonal utility increase feels separate from a subscription cluster. Each event seems temporary and situational.

But repeated temporary events can form a permanent pattern.

A household may describe borrowed capacity as temporary for years if shortfalls continue appearing before prior balances fully clear. The term "temporary" becomes misleading when the need for temporary support keeps repeating.

Patterns matter more than isolated incidents.

If revolving balances repeatedly absorb timing gaps, the issue is not one timing gap. It is flow misalignment.

If irregular expenses repeatedly move onto credit, the issue is not one repair. It is weak shock absorption.

If repayment progress repeatedly reverses after aggressive payment periods, the issue may be repayment capacity.

If new obligations continue appearing through financed replacements and recurring services, baseline inflation may still be active.

Debt mapping makes these patterns more visible. Pressure ranking helps clarify which sources create the most instability. But leakage interruption requires seeing not only the balances that exist, but the pathways through which new balances continue entering the system.

This visibility changes the meaning of progress.

Progress is not only a declining balance.

Progress is also fewer shortfalls converting into debt.

Progress is less reliance on revolving balances for timing coordination.

Progress is improved liquidity recovery after irregular expenses.

Progress is slower obligation regeneration.

Progress is a household structure that no longer requires borrowed capacity as frequently to preserve ordinary continuity.

This kind of progress is often quieter than rapid payoff. It may not appear as dramatic from month to month. But structurally, it is essential because it reduces the system's tendency to recreate the same pressure repeatedly.

Leakage interruption is usually gradual.

It rarely occurs through one dramatic reset. More often, the household becomes less dependent on borrowed continuity over time. One category of recurring shortfall becomes less frequent. One timing gap becomes easier to absorb. One irregular expense does not become a new balance. Liquidity recovers slightly faster after disruption. Repayment continues without immediate reversal. New obligations form more slowly.

The structure begins to retain improvement.

This is the difference between a system that only repays and a system that stabilizes.

A repayment-only system may show movement while remaining vulnerable to constant regeneration. A stabilizing system reduces existing obligations while also slowing the creation of new ones. Debt pressure weakens because the household is no longer fighting the same shortfalls in repeated form.

This also reduces fatigue.

When debt keeps reforming, the household experiences repayment as a recurring restart. Progress feels temporary. Effort feels fragile. The same balances or similar balances keep returning. Over time, this can make debt reduction feel ineffective even when the household is applying real effort.

Leakage interruption improves the emotional environment indirectly by improving the operating environment directly. The household no longer depends as heavily on perfect conditions. Ordinary irregularity becomes more absorbable. Timing gaps become less destabilizing. Fewer disruptions become new obligations. The structure becomes easier to coordinate because it is no longer constantly regenerating pressure underneath repayment.

Again, the goal is not rigid control over every expense.

Households are not machines. Ordinary life contains uneven costs, imperfect timing, and changing conditions. Stability does not require eliminating irregularity. It requires enough flexibility to keep irregularity from repeatedly becoming future obligation pressure.

That is why leakage interruption belongs inside the debt stability system.

Repayment matters. Existing obligations must decline for pressure to weaken. But repayment cannot carry the entire burden if the household structure continues producing new shortfalls beneath it.

Debt pressure weakens meaningfully when two movements occur together: old obligations decline, and new obligation creation slows.

At that point, repayment begins to hold.

Liquidity has more room to recover. Runway begins to lengthen. Payment tolerance improves because recurring pressure is no longer constantly expanding. Accumulation drag loses some force as fewer balances remain active or reforming. Flow misalignment becomes easier to manage because fewer obligations compete against income timing. Shock conversion becomes less frequent because reserves have more opportunity to absorb disruption directly.

The household does not become stable because nothing ever goes wrong.

It becomes more stable because fewer ordinary disruptions become debt.

Leakage interruption is therefore not a spending lecture. It is a structural condition for repayment durability.

A household can make payments for years and still remain unstable if recurring shortfalls continuously recreate future obligations. But once the pathways of regeneration begin narrowing, repayment starts doing something more powerful than reducing balances. It begins restoring flexibility that stays inside the system long enough to support long-term recovery.

Creating Payment Stability

Many households interpret payment instability as a discipline problem.

A payment arrives late, an overdraft appears, a balance expands unexpectedly, or a draft collides with another obligation, and the experience is often framed internally as disorganization, carelessness, or lack of control. The household may feel as though it is constantly reacting, constantly adjusting, constantly trying to stay ahead of obligations that never seem to arrive at manageable times.

But many payment problems emerge from structural misalignment rather than unwillingness to pay.

A household may be trying consistently to maintain continuity while still experiencing recurring timing strain because the payment structure itself does not fit the household's actual operating rhythm.

Income may arrive unevenly.

Due dates may cluster aggressively.

Automatic drafts may process before inflow clears.

Variable bills may collide with fixed obligations.

Payment amounts may exceed realistic operating margin during certain periods of the month even if they appear manageable across the month as a whole.

The structure may therefore create pressure through timing, coordination, and sequencing rather than through outright inability alone.

This is where obligation alignment becomes important.

Obligation Alignment is the process of arranging debt payments, due dates, payment amounts, income timing, and recurring systems so obligations fit more cleanly inside the household's cash-flow structure.

Alignment does not eliminate debt pressure.

It reduces unnecessary coordination pressure.

That distinction matters because many households operate under constant timing strain even when total monthly income is theoretically sufficient to support ordinary obligations. The instability appears not because the structure lacks income entirely, but because obligations and inflow move through the month in conflicting patterns.

Debt payments are not experienced only as amounts.

They are experienced as timing demands.

The same payment can feel stable or destabilizing depending on when it arrives relative to income, reserves, and other obligations already competing for available cash flow.

A payment scheduled shortly after income arrives may feel manageable because liquidity is temporarily strongest. The same payment occurring days earlier, after several other obligations have already processed, may create short-term compression severe enough to trigger substitution pressure or timing instability.

This is why timing cannot be separated from repayment stability.

A household may technically earn enough money across a month while still experiencing recurring operational strain because obligations concentrate at points where available liquidity remains temporarily weak.

Clustered due dates are one of the clearest examples.

Several obligations may arrive during the same narrow period:

a vehicle payment,

multiple credit card minimums,

insurance drafts,

subscription renewals,

utilities,

and financing payments operating simultaneously within a compressed portion of the month.

If income arrives later, or arrives unevenly through variable work schedules, commissions, contract timing, or inconsistent hours, the structure may experience temporary compression even if total income remains adequate over longer periods.

This creates an important distinction between total affordability and operational survivability.

A payment may be affordable in theory while remaining unstable in practice because it arrives at the wrong point inside the household's cash-flow rhythm.

This timing pressure increases coordination load.

Households under debt pressure often carry enormous coordination responsibility even when no obvious crisis is visible externally. They must continuously track due dates, minimums, drafts, balances, paycheck timing, liquidity levels, irregular expenses, and sequencing decisions simply to preserve continuity.

When alignment is poor, coordination itself becomes exhausting.

The household spends substantial attention preventing timing failures rather than rebuilding stability underneath the system.

This is one reason debt pressure often feels mentally consuming even when balances are not expanding dramatically at the moment. The structure demands constant operational monitoring because timing friction exists everywhere inside the payment environment.

A paycheck arrives and immediately must be allocated across clustered obligations.

A delayed deposit creates sequencing pressure.

A draft processes earlier than expected.

A variable utility bill collides with an existing payment week.

An irregular expense interrupts the timing structure temporarily.

The household responds reactively, attempting to preserve continuity one timing decision at a time.

Over long periods, this coordination burden becomes destabilizing in itself because reactive sequencing consumes flexibility continuously.

Poor alignment therefore creates pressure beyond the balances themselves.

It creates friction.

And friction matters operationally because friction increases the amount of effort required simply to keep the system functioning normally.

This becomes especially visible when due-date clustering compresses obligations into narrow windows.

A household may possess enough total income to satisfy all monthly obligations eventually, yet still experience overdrafts, revolving substitution, delayed payments, or liquidity strain because too many obligations compete for cash flow simultaneously before inflow has fully stabilized.

The problem is not always the total burden.

Sometimes the problem is the shape of the burden across time.

A household operating under dense clustering often experiences recurring short-term compression even during otherwise stable periods. Liquidity becomes temporarily exhausted. Timing gaps widen. Flexibility narrows. Short-term borrowing becomes more likely because obligations concentrate faster than cash flow replenishes.

This can create the misleading appearance that the household is fundamentally incapable of supporting the obligations when, in reality, the structure may simply be poorly aligned operationally.

The distinction matters because timing instability often produces avoidable pressure.

The household may repeatedly rely on revolving balances not because income is catastrophically insufficient, but because obligations and inflow collide in ways that force temporary substitution repeatedly.

This connects directly to earlier discussions of flow misalignment.

Income variability becomes far more destabilizing when obligations are rigidly concentrated. A household with uneven inflow but flexible timing structures may remain relatively stable. The same income pattern operating against dense clusters of fixed drafts and obligations may produce recurring instability despite similar overall earnings.

Automatic systems interact with this dynamic in complicated ways.

Automatic payments can stabilize household operation when they fit the cash-flow structure properly. They can reduce missed sequencing, simplify coordination, and preserve continuity by reducing the amount of manual attention required for recurring obligations.

But automatic systems are only stabilizing when they align with actual operating conditions.

An automatic draft processing before income clears may create unnecessary compression.

Several drafts clustering together may increase short-term liquidity strain.

Automatic systems operating without sufficient reserve support may amplify fragility because timing errors become immediate rather than adjustable.

This is not an argument against automation.

It is an argument for structural fit.

Automatic systems are not inherently stabilizing or destabilizing. Their effect depends on whether they operate inside a payment structure aligned with income timing, reserve capacity, obligation density, and operational rhythm.

A household may therefore appear organized externally while remaining structurally fragile underneath if the timing architecture itself remains poorly coordinated.

This becomes even more important when payment amounts exceed repayment capacity.

Earlier chapters established that repayment plans destabilize when they absorb too much operating margin relative to actual household conditions. Payment alignment interacts directly with this principle because repayment structures that ignore timing reality may create instability even if the household is committed to repayment progress.

A payment amount may look reasonable mathematically while remaining operationally disruptive because it compresses liquidity too aggressively at certain points in the month.

This distinction is important because repayment systems do not exist in abstract calculations.

They exist inside moving operational environments where income timing, irregular expenses, reserve levels, and obligation density all interact continuously.

A repayment structure therefore succeeds not merely because the payments are technically affordable, but because the payments remain survivable across ordinary variability.

Alignment improves survivability.

When obligations fit more realistically inside household rhythm, coordination pressure decreases. The structure becomes easier to operate consistently because timing friction weakens.

This reduction in friction matters more than many households initially realize.

Friction creates instability gradually.

A system requiring constant emergency coordination remains vulnerable because even small disruptions can interrupt sequencing and trigger cascading pressure elsewhere in the structure.

Reducing friction therefore improves stability even before balances decline dramatically.

Fewer timing surprises emerge.

Liquidity strain becomes less compressed.

Avoidable late pressure weakens.

Reactive borrowing becomes less frequent.

The household spends less attention preventing operational collisions and more attention rebuilding flexibility underneath ordinary operation.

Importantly, alignment does not solve debt independently.

A well-aligned structure can still contain heavy obligation load, accumulation drag, or elevated baseline pressure. But poor alignment magnifies all of those pressures unnecessarily by adding coordination instability on top of existing financial strain.

This is why obligation alignment supports earlier mechanisms throughout the debt system.

Flow misalignment becomes less disruptive when obligations fit more realistically against income rhythm.

Payment tolerance improves when recurring obligations distribute more evenly instead of clustering aggressively.

Leakage interruption becomes easier because fewer short-term timing gaps convert into borrowing triggers.

Maintenance trap dynamics become more visible because the structure is easier to observe clearly once timing chaos decreases.

Pressure ranking improves because obligations can be evaluated more coherently when constant sequencing emergencies stop dominating attention.

The broader effect is not perfection.

It is operational calm.

That calm matters because households operating under constant timing pressure often experience every obligation as urgent simultaneously. The system becomes emotionally loud because coordination strain never fully subsides. Every payment feels risky. Every timing shift threatens disruption. Every irregular expense competes against already compressed sequencing structures.

When alignment improves, some of that noise weakens.

The household still carries obligations.

The balances may still require long recovery periods.

Repayment may still move gradually.

But the structure becomes easier to inhabit because fewer avoidable collisions are occurring continuously inside ordinary operation.

This distinction helps explain why payment instability should not automatically be interpreted morally.

A household can be attentive, responsible, and highly effortful while still struggling under poorly aligned timing structures. Many payment problems emerge not because the household refuses to pay, but because obligations move through the system in ways that create unnecessary operational compression.

Understanding this reduces shame while improving structural interpretation.

The household does not necessarily need perfect discipline.

Often it needs better fit.

Better fit between due dates and income rhythm.

Better fit between repayment intensity and operating margin.

Better fit between automatic systems and actual reserve conditions.

Better fit between obligation timing and the realities of ordinary household variability.

Because repayment becomes more stable when the structure itself stops fighting the household's operating rhythm constantly.

This is one of the quieter forms of stabilization inside debt systems.

Nothing dramatic changes externally at first. Balances may still exist. Obligations may still require years of gradual reduction. But coordination becomes less chaotic. Timing pressure softens. Reactive sequencing declines. The structure becomes more survivable because ordinary operation requires less constant emergency adjustment.

That survivability matters.

A repayment structure that fits the household's actual cash-flow rhythm can continue functioning through ordinary variability much more effectively than one dependent on constant perfect coordination. And over time, that reduction in avoidable friction often matters as much as repayment effort itself because stability improves not only through balance reduction, but through the ability to operate month after month without continuous timing strain overwhelming the system.

Building a Debt Buffer

Households under debt pressure often experience a difficult tension once repayment becomes serious.

Balances feel urgent. Interest continues accumulating. Minimum payments remain active. Obligation load continues compressing flexibility month after month. After long periods of financial strain, it can feel emotionally obvious that every available dollar should move directly toward debt reduction as quickly as possible.

The logic appears reasonable.

If debt creates pressure, then faster repayment should create faster relief.

And in many situations, aggressive repayment does reduce balances more quickly. Statements decline faster. Repayment timelines shorten. Visible progress becomes easier to measure. The household feels movement instead of stagnation.

But debt systems do not operate in isolation from ordinary instability.

Repayment occurs inside real household conditions where repairs still happen, income still fluctuates, expenses still arrive unevenly, and timing shocks still appear without warning.

When repayment eliminates all remaining liquidity, even small disruptions can reverse progress quickly.

A vehicle repair arrives after several months of aggressive repayment. A delayed paycheck creates temporary timing compression. A medical bill interrupts sequencing. Reduced work hours weaken monthly cash flow unexpectedly. An appliance replacement appears before reserves recover.

The household had been reducing debt successfully.

Then the disruption converts directly into new borrowing because no shock absorption capacity remained underneath the repayment structure itself.

This is why repayment alone does not determine durability.

The structure surrounding repayment matters just as much.

Protective Liquidity is the reserve capacity that protects repayment progress by absorbing ordinary shocks before they become new debt.

This is an important distinction because protective liquidity is often misunderstood as avoidance of repayment or hesitation about reducing balances.

That is not the mechanism operating here.

Protective liquidity is not repayment avoidance.

It is protection around repayment.

Its role is not to eliminate debt directly. Its role is to reduce the likelihood that ordinary instability recreates debt faster than repayment can reduce it.

This becomes especially important after earlier chapters established how repayment capacity, leakage interruption, shock conversion, and obligation alignment interact across the broader household system.

Aggressive repayment can reduce balances quickly.

But if aggressive repayment leaves the structure with no reserve capacity, the household may become operationally brittle. The repayment structure appears efficient during stable periods because balances decline rapidly. Yet the absence of liquidity underneath the system means ordinary disruptions become far more dangerous.

A structure without shock absorption often appears stable right up until disruption occurs.

That disruption does not need to be catastrophic.

A repair.

A deductible.

A temporary income delay.

A timing mismatch.

An irregular utility spike.

A household expense that arrives earlier than expected.

When liquidity has been compressed too aggressively, these ordinary events frequently recreate obligation pressure immediately.

This is one reason many households experience debt repayment as repetitive rather than cumulative.

Balances decline.

A disruption appears.

Borrowing returns.

The repayment process restarts.

The issue is not necessarily lack of commitment.

Often the structure simply lacked enough absorption capacity to preserve progress through ordinary variability.

Protective liquidity changes this dynamic because it interrupts shock conversion before instability becomes new debt.

A small reserve can absorb timing instability directly instead of forcing revolving substitution. A repair may reduce reserves temporarily, but it does not automatically become a future repayment obligation. A delayed paycheck may compress liquidity temporarily, but it does not necessarily require new borrowing to preserve continuity.

The disruption still exists.

But the disruption remains contained instead of becoming embedded into the future obligation structure.

This distinction matters enormously for long-term stabilization.

Without reserve capacity, repayment progress becomes highly interruption-sensitive. The structure depends on uninterrupted conditions remaining stable long enough for balances to decline. Real household systems rarely behave that cleanly across extended periods.

Income shifts.

Repairs appear.

Seasonal costs fluctuate.

Medical expenses emerge unevenly.

Life introduces instability repeatedly.

When every disruption recreates debt, repayment struggles to accumulate lasting structural improvement because obligation load continuously regenerates underneath the repayment process.

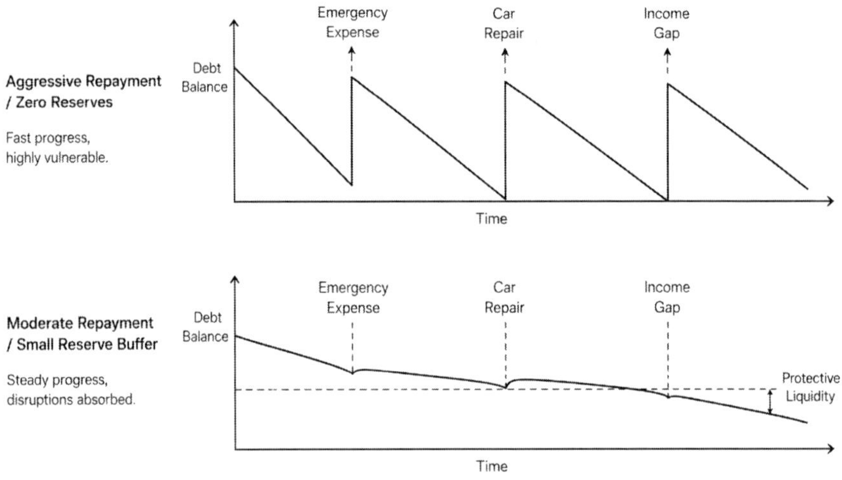

[Figure 8: Protective Liquidity Around Debt Repayment]

Protective liquidity therefore functions less like excess accumulation and more like operational insulation.

It creates enough separation between ordinary instability and future borrowing that repayment has time to hold.

This is why a small reserve can sometimes stabilize repayment more effectively than maximum repayment intensity with no buffer underneath it.

A household aggressively directing every available dollar toward balances may reduce debt faster temporarily while simultaneously weakening its ability to survive ordinary disruption. Another household preserving modest reserve capacity while reducing balances more gradually may appear slower externally while building a repayment structure that survives interruption more effectively.

The difference becomes visible after instability appears.

In the first structure, a disruption frequently recreates borrowing immediately because no absorption layer exists between the event and future obligation formation.

In the second structure, reserves may absorb the instability directly, allowing repayment progress to continue without complete reversal.

This does not mean protective liquidity requires indefinite hesitation or endless reserve accumulation before repayment begins. That would create a different imbalance where repayment slows unnecessarily while obligations remain active for extended periods.

The issue is functional absorption capacity.

Too little liquidity creates fragility.

Too much reluctance to reduce obligations can preserve pressure unnecessarily.

Protective liquidity exists between those extremes. It is not about hoarding cash indefinitely. It is about maintaining enough accessible flexibility that ordinary household instability does not continuously erase repayment progress.

This is particularly important because many debt systems already operate under compressed conditions before repayment intensifies.

Runway may already be short.

Payment tolerance may already be narrow.

Flow misalignment may already create recurring timing pressure.

Accumulation drag may already slow flexibility recovery.

Leakage interruption may still be incomplete.

Under these conditions, eliminating all reserve capacity can intensify vulnerability faster than balances decline.

The household becomes dependent on perfect continuity.

And perfect continuity is rarely available for long periods inside ordinary life.

Protective liquidity reduces this dependency by extending the structure's ability to absorb irregularity without immediately creating new obligations.

This connects directly to shock conversion.

Earlier chapters explained that many balances originate not from dramatic overspending but from ordinary disruptions interacting with insufficient reserves. A vehicle repair becomes revolving debt. Medical costs become payment plans. Temporary income instability expands existing balances.

Protective liquidity interrupts that conversion process.

The disruption may still reduce available reserves temporarily, but it does not necessarily create another recurring future claim against income.

This is also why protective liquidity supports repayment capacity.

Repayment structures fail when they exceed the household's ability to maintain continuity during ordinary instability. A reserve helps repayment survive disruption because the system no longer relies entirely on uninterrupted income and perfect sequencing.

The repayment process therefore becomes more durable.

Durability matters more than temporary intensity.

A repayment structure that survives irregularity consistently often improves long-term stability more effectively than one that produces rapid reduction briefly before repeated reversal cycles begin.

Protective liquidity also interacts with obligation alignment.

Timing pressure weakens when reserves exist underneath the payment structure. A delayed deposit becomes less destabilizing. A clustered due-date period becomes more survivable. Automatic drafts become less fragile because temporary liquidity gaps no longer immediately threaten continuity.

This reduction in timing sensitivity improves coordination quality throughout the household system.

It also weakens substitution pressure.

Without reserves, ordinary shortfalls frequently default toward revolving balances because the structure lacks another absorption mechanism. With protective liquidity, some of those same shortfalls can remain temporary operational disruptions rather than becoming new obligation load.

This reduces the frequency of recurring debt regeneration.

That distinction matters because repayment progress depends not only on reducing old balances, but on slowing the formation of new ones simultaneously.

Protective liquidity therefore supports leakage interruption directly.

It gives the household more opportunity to absorb irregularity before shortfalls recreate future obligations.

The emotional effect of this should also be acknowledged carefully, though not exaggerated.

A household operating with no reserves often experiences repayment as fragile because any disruption threatens immediate reversal. Every repair feels dangerous. Every delayed paycheck creates pressure. Every irregular expense threatens to erase progress that required months to create.

This produces ongoing tension because the structure remains highly interruption-sensitive.

A modest reserve changes the operating environment.

Not because instability disappears, but because instability becomes more survivable.

The household may still encounter repairs, medical costs, reduced hours, or irregular expenses. But those events no longer automatically threaten to recreate obligation load immediately. The repayment process therefore feels less brittle because the structure possesses at least some shock absorption capacity underneath ordinary operation.

That calmer operating condition matters structurally.

The household becomes less reactive.

Timing coordination improves.

Pressure concentration weakens modestly.

Repayment continuity becomes easier to preserve across ordinary variability.

Importantly, this chapter is not arguing that liquidity alone solves debt pressure.

Balances still matter.

Obligation load still compresses flexibility.

Accumulation drag still extends timelines.

Repayment still requires sustained operating capacity across time.

But repayment becomes more durable when liquidity protection and debt reduction operate together instead of competing against one another destructively.

This is one reason highly aggressive repayment structures sometimes fail despite strong commitment. The household focuses entirely on balance reduction while unintentionally removing the very shock absorption capacity needed to preserve repayment continuity through ordinary instability.

The result is often cyclical:

aggressive reduction,
shock exposure,
new borrowing,
reversal,
restart.

Protective liquidity weakens that cycle by reducing how often instability converts into future debt.

Over time, this changes the shape of recovery itself.

Repayment no longer depends entirely on perfect conditions.

The household can absorb some variability without collapsing repayment momentum immediately.

Progress becomes steadier because the structure itself becomes more survivable.

That survivability is one of the quiet foundations of debt stability.

The goal is not maximum repayment aggression at every moment regardless of operating conditions. The goal is a repayment structure capable of surviving ordinary shocks long enough for flexibility, liquidity, and stability to rebuild gradually across time.

When repayment and protective liquidity work together, progress has a greater chance of remaining inside the household system instead of repeatedly being erased by the next interruption waiting just beyond the current payment cycle.

Choosing a Repayment Order

Once a household begins reducing debt more deliberately, a natural question eventually appears.

Which obligation should be addressed first?

At first, the question seems straightforward. If balances exist simultaneously, then repayment must begin somewhere. The difficulty emerges when the household discovers that different debts create different forms of pressure, and those pressures do not always align neatly with universal payoff rules.

One balance may carry heavy interest accumulation. Another may generate large monthly payment strain. Another may create constant psychological pressure. Another may threaten transportation continuity if disrupted. Another may repeatedly destabilize timing coordination across the month.

The balances exist together, but they do not behave identically inside the household system.

Common debt advice often tries to simplify this complexity through universal sequencing methods.

One approach prioritizes the smallest balance first. Another focuses on the highest interest rate. Another centers emotional relief. Another reacts to whichever obligation feels most urgent in the moment.

Each of these approaches identifies something real.

A smaller balance may improve momentum.

A high-interest balance may create substantial accumulation drag.

An emotionally exhausting obligation may consume attention constantly.

An urgent account may require immediate stabilization to preserve continuity.

But none of these methods captures the entire operating structure by itself.

This is why repayment sequencing cannot be understood purely through ideology or universal formulas.

The household system is more complex than a single repayment variable.

Sequenced Reduction is the process of ordering debt reduction according to the household's actual pressure profile rather than a universal repayment rule.

The important distinction is that repayment order exists to reduce instability in a way the household can sustain operationally.

It is not a test of discipline.

It is not ideological purity.

It is not proof that one method is universally correct and another universally flawed.

It is a structural interpretation problem.

Different debts create different forms of compression across liquidity, timing, attention, flexibility, continuity, and long-term recovery.

The sequence matters because the order determines which pressures weaken first.

Universal payoff systems often simplify this complexity because simplification feels manageable under stress. A household already carrying heavy coordination load may understandably want one clear answer that removes ambiguity.

Pay the smallest first.

Pay the highest interest first.

Pay the most emotionally painful first.

Pay the most urgent first.

Each approach provides a usable framework. But each framework also highlights one dimension of pressure while potentially overlooking others.

A smallest-balance approach may reduce visible account count and improve psychological momentum while leaving larger recurring payment strain largely unchanged. A household may eliminate several small balances successfully yet continue operating under severe liquidity compression because a larger obligation still absorbs too much monthly cash flow.

A highest-interest approach may reduce long-term accumulation drag effectively while ignoring timing congestion, continuity risk, or recurring operational friction elsewhere in the structure. A mathematically expensive balance may matter greatly over time while another obligation creates more immediate instability through payment size or coordination pressure.

An emotion-first approach may reduce mental exhaustion and avoidance behavior, which absolutely matters operationally. But emotional intensity does not always correspond perfectly with structural compression. The loudest balance psychologically may not be the obligation creating the greatest liquidity strain or disruption sensitivity.

An urgency-first approach may preserve continuity during active instability, but reactive urgency can also trap households inside constant short-term firefighting where sequencing changes repeatedly without improving broader structural stability.

None of these perspectives is entirely wrong.

They are incomplete lenses.

The household system itself is multidimensional.

This is why pressure profile becomes more important than any universal repayment doctrine.

A pressure profile is the combined pattern of payment size, interest drag, timing strain, risk exposure, continuity importance, liquidity compression, and psychological load attached to each obligation.

Each debt creates its own pressure signature inside the system.

Some balances are expensive primarily because interest extends repayment duration aggressively.

Some create pressure because the minimum payment absorbs too much monthly operating margin.

Some create recurring timing friction because the due date collides badly with income rhythm.

Some carry continuity importance because they are connected to transportation, housing stability, or critical household infrastructure.

Some generate constant psychological noise that weakens decision clarity and increases avoidance behavior.

Some repeatedly regenerate through substitution pressure because they remain tied to recurring operational gaps.

Others appear large on paper while creating relatively modest operational instability because their payment structure fits comfortably inside the household's existing cash-flow rhythm.

The balance alone therefore cannot fully explain the pressure.

The household must understand how the obligation behaves operationally.

A high minimum payment, for example, may compress liquidity more aggressively than a higher-interest obligation with a smaller recurring burden. A debt tied to transportation continuity may carry disproportionate operational importance because disruption could affect income reliability itself. A cluster of smaller recurring obligations may create substantial coordination load despite individually manageable balances because the combined timing structure continuously strains liquidity sequencing.

An emotionally exhausting account may also matter more structurally than it appears mathematically if it dominates attention constantly, weakens clarity, or contributes to reactive financial behavior across the broader system.

The point is not to prescribe one universally correct sequence.

The point is to recognize that repayment order affects multiple forms of stability simultaneously.

	Payment Size	Interest	Stress Load	Instability Risk	Cash-Flow Burden	Pressure Rank
Debt A	◒	●	●	◒	●	1 (Highest)
Debt B	○	◒	◒	●	◒	2
Debt C	●	○	○	◒	○	3
Debt D	◒	○	◒	○	◒	4 (Lowest)

Legend: ○ = Low ◒ = Medium ● = High

Sequence by pressure profile, not balance alone.

[Figure 9: Pressure-Based Debt Sequencing]

Once the household begins interpreting obligations through pressure profile instead of isolated balance logic, sequencing becomes less ideological and more operational.

The question shifts.

Not:

Which method is universally best?

But:

Which pressures are destabilizing this household most aggressively right now?

This distinction matters because households under pressure often sequence repayment reactively rather than structurally.

Whichever creditor calls most aggressively receives attention first.

Whichever balance feels most embarrassing dominates focus.

Whichever account creates immediate anxiety absorbs available liquidity.

Whichever payment was most recently missed becomes the center of attention temporarily.

This is understandable. Debt pressure creates noise. When every obligation feels urgent simultaneously, the household often responds emotionally to whichever pressure signal feels loudest in the moment.

But reactive sequencing can leave deeper structural compression untouched.

A household may repeatedly redirect resources toward whichever balance creates immediate emotional discomfort while leaving liquidity strain, timing congestion, or recurring substitution pressure largely unchanged underneath.

The system remains unstable because sequencing is being driven by emotional volume rather than operational interpretation.

Debt mapping and pressure ranking earlier in the book were important precisely because they reduced this fragmentation.

Once obligations become visible together, the household can begin seeing how different balances affect different parts of the structure simultaneously.

One obligation may compress runway heavily.

Another may create recurring timing instability.

Another may extend accumulation drag across long periods.

Another may repeatedly regenerate through leakage patterns.

Another may threaten continuity if disrupted.

Sequenced reduction becomes possible only after this visibility exists.

Without visibility, sequencing often becomes reactive.

With visibility, sequencing becomes interpretable.

Importantly, sequencing alone still cannot stabilize the system if repayment intensity exceeds repayment capacity.

A theoretically excellent priority structure can still fail if the repayment approach destroys liquidity, compresses operating margin too aggressively, or weakens shock absorption underneath ordinary household operation.

The sequence itself must remain survivable.

A household directing overwhelming pressure toward one balance while eliminating all reserve capacity may reduce that obligation temporarily while recreating instability elsewhere through substitution pressure or shock conversion.

This is why sequencing cannot be separated from repayment capacity.

The best repayment order still fails if the structure carrying the repayment effort becomes too fragile to survive ordinary disruption.

Protective liquidity matters here as well.

A sequence that appears mathematically efficient but leaves the household operationally brittle may reverse quickly after instability appears. A repair, delayed paycheck, medical expense, or timing disruption can erase progress rapidly when the repayment structure lacks enough absorption capacity underneath it.

This means sequencing should reduce instability while preserving survivability.

Not maximum aggression.

Not ideological purity.

Not rigid loyalty to a universal method regardless of household conditions.

Survivability.

The household must be able to continue operating while the sequence unfolds across time.

This also explains why sequencing changes.

Pressure profiles evolve.

A balance creating severe liquidity compression today may matter less later after other obligations decline. Timing strain may improve once certain recurring payments disappear. Protective liquidity may strengthen enough that previous coordination problems weaken. Income rhythm may stabilize. A psychologically exhausting account may stop dominating attention once visibility improves elsewhere.

The structure changes.

Therefore the pressure profile changes.

A sequence that made sense under one operating condition may become less relevant later as the household stabilizes gradually.

This is not inconsistency.

It is governance awareness.

A rigid sequence that ignores evolving conditions can become as destabilizing as reactive sequencing because it stops interpreting the actual structure and instead obeys a fixed rule disconnected from current operational reality.

Good sequencing remains responsive to the household system itself.

This responsiveness is one reason repayment sequencing should not become ideological.

Different households experience different forms of instability.

A household with strong income continuity but severe timing congestion may need different sequencing logic than a household with thin liquidity and recurring shock conversion. A structure operating under high accumulation drag may experience pressure differently than one dominated by large recurring payment strain. A household with stable cash flow but intense psychological avoidance may require different sequencing considerations than one dealing primarily with substitution pressure and operational leakage.

The repayment order must therefore reflect the structure that actually exists.

Not the structure imagined by a universal formula.

This chapter is not arguing against simple repayment methods entirely. Simplicity can reduce paralysis. Clear frameworks can improve coordination. Momentum matters. Emotional relief matters. Long-term interest drag matters.

But no single variable fully defines instability.

The household system contains multiple forms of pressure interacting simultaneously.

Sequenced reduction becomes useful because it acknowledges that debt is not only a balance problem.

It is a pressure-distribution problem.

The order determines which pressures weaken first.

A sequence reducing recurring liquidity compression may improve flexibility more quickly than one focused purely on mathematical efficiency. A sequence reducing timing strain may improve survivability more than one focused only on visible account elimination. A sequence protecting continuity infrastructure may preserve income reliability itself. A sequence reducing psychologically exhausting obligations may improve coordination quality across the broader system.

Each sequence reshapes the structure differently.

This is why repayment order matters.

Not because one universal method always wins, but because sequencing determines how pressure exits the household system over time.

And the most stable repayment structures are usually the ones that reduce instability in an order the household can continue surviving long enough to complete.

Debt Fatigue and Decision Pressure

Chapter 17 — Debt Fatigue and Decision Pressure

Debt pressure does not operate only through balances, payments, or interest. Over long periods, it also affects attention.

A household carrying debt for months or years must continue coordinating an ongoing operating structure. Payments must be tracked. Liquidity must be protected. Due dates must be managed. Irregular expenses must be absorbed. Timing gaps must be navigated. New instability must be prevented while old obligations are still being reduced.

Even when progress is occurring, the system continues requiring management.

This creates a form of pressure that develops gradually rather than dramatically.

Control Depletion is the gradual weakening of attention, patience, coordination quality, and decision capacity that occurs when debt pressure requires sustained management over long periods.

The important distinction is that control depletion is not evidence of irresponsibility or lack of effort. It is a predictable structural response to prolonged operating pressure.

A household can care deeply about improving its finances and still become fatigued by the ongoing coordination required to maintain progress across extended repayment timelines.

The issue is not motivation alone.

The issue is duration.

Debt reduction often unfolds more slowly than households initially expect. Balances may decline, but not quickly. Liquidity may improve, but gradually. Obligations may shrink, but remain active for long periods. Maintenance pressure continues while the structure is still stabilizing underneath.

Progress may be real while pressure still feels present.

A household may continue making payments consistently month after month while still experiencing narrow margins, ongoing timing coordination, and recurring disruption sensitivity. The balances move downward, but the operating environment may still require constant attention.

This is one reason long repayment periods feel heavier than many households expect.

The household is not only reducing balances. It is sustaining coordination effort continuously across time.

A family paying down revolving balances for two years may technically be improving throughout the entire period. Yet during those same years, repairs still occur. Income still fluctuates. Expenses still cluster unexpectedly. Due dates still arrive every month. Payment sequencing still matters. Liquidity still requires protection.

Improvement does not automatically remove management demand immediately.

This distinction matters because many repayment models quietly assume that progress itself will generate enough emotional momentum to carry the household indefinitely. But long-duration systems do not operate primarily on momentum. They operate on sustainability.

A short burst of repayment intensity may feel powerful temporarily. A household may direct substantial energy toward debt reduction for several months after a period of stress or financial clarity. Spending tightens. Extra payments increase. Attention sharpens.

But prolonged systems behave differently from short-term efforts.

Over time, attention fluctuates. Conditions change. Unexpected instability interrupts routines. Financial pressure competes with ordinary household life. The coordination burden remains active long after the initial urgency fades.

This is where control depletion begins appearing operationally.

The household may still intend to improve. But sustained pressure gradually weakens the ability to maintain the same level of constant coordination indefinitely.

The process often develops quietly.

Balances decline slowly enough that improvement feels delayed. Payments continue leaving every month, yet obligations remain visible. Liquidity may still feel fragile despite progress. Small disruptions continue threatening sequencing stability. The household may feel caught between improvement and persistence simultaneously.

The result is not necessarily collapse.

More often, it is exhaustion.

Not dramatic exhaustion.

Operational exhaustion.

The kind that develops when every month still requires careful attention long after the household expected pressure to ease more noticeably.

This is why debt fatigue frequently appears even inside systems that are technically improving.

The household is not failing.

The household is carrying prolonged coordination load.

This distinction becomes especially important when discussing avoidance.

Avoidance is often interpreted simplistically as denial, irresponsibility, or lack of discipline. But in many debt structures, avoidance develops because the system itself feels persistently heavy.

A household may avoid checking balances because progress feels too slow relative to effort. It may delay reviewing statements because every review reinforces how long repayment still appears likely to continue. It may stop interpreting the debt map clearly because constant visibility without enough immediate relief becomes emotionally draining over time.

This does not mean the household stopped caring.

It means the structure continues demanding attention without producing enough visible reduction in pressure fast enough to sustain constant engagement comfortably.

Repeated reversals intensify this effect.

A household may make meaningful progress for several months, then encounter a repair, income interruption, medical cost, or timing disruption that partially rebuilds balances again. The structure improves, destabilizes temporarily, then improves again.

Even when the overall trajectory remains better than before, repeated interruptions weaken the sense of control continuity.

The household begins questioning whether progress will hold.

Not because improvement is impossible, but because instability repeatedly interrupts visible momentum.

This creates decision pressure.

Under long repayment timelines, ordinary financial choices begin carrying disproportionate weight because operating margin remains narrow.

A small expense may feel consequential because liquidity is still rebuilding.

A timing mistake may create cascading coordination problems.

An irregular bill may threaten repayment rhythm.

A delayed paycheck may force difficult sequencing decisions.

The household begins operating inside an environment where small variations appear amplified.

This increases attention strain because the system leaves little room for disengagement.

The structure still functions, but it functions conditionally.

Attention remains required.

Coordination remains required.

Monitoring remains required.

And over long periods, this sustained requirement can weaken decision quality gradually.

Not because the household becomes careless, but because prolonged pressure consumes cognitive bandwidth continuously.

This is one reason intensity alone rarely sustains long repayment periods effectively.

Intensity depends on maintaining unusually high levels of focus, restriction, coordination, and emotional urgency for extended durations. But real household systems contain variability.

Repairs occur.

Schedules change.

Income fluctuates.

Children get sick.

Work hours shift.

Appliances fail.

Unexpected travel appears.

Administrative mistakes happen.

Energy levels fluctuate.

Attention fluctuates.

No household maintains maximum operational focus permanently.

A repayment structure requiring constant intensity therefore becomes fragile over time because it assumes conditions that ordinary life rarely sustains consistently.

This is why many aggressive repayment efforts eventually destabilize despite strong intentions.

The issue is not necessarily commitment.

The issue is that the repayment environment itself may require more sustained coordination than the household can realistically maintain across long timelines.

Sustainable control becomes more important than temporary intensity.

Sustainable control is a repayment environment where progress can continue without requiring constant panic, perfect coordination, or uninterrupted emotional urgency.

Stable systems reduce dependency on maximum attention over time.

Protective liquidity helps because disruptions stop threatening immediate reversal constantly. Obligation alignment helps because timing strain weakens. Reduced leakage lowers recurring substitution pressure. Repayment capacity prevents the system from becoming too brittle during reduction efforts. Pressure-based sequencing reduces destabilizing obligations in more survivable ways.

Together, these changes reduce the amount of continuous emergency coordination required to keep the structure functioning.

This is one of the deeper meanings of stabilization.

Not merely balance reduction.

Reduction in control load.

A household under severe instability must constantly interpret pressure signals. Which payment comes first? Which bill can wait temporarily? Which expense creates risk? Which balance is expanding? Which timing gap requires coordination? Which obligation threatens continuity?

The structure demands constant active management.

As stability improves gradually, some of this management burden begins weakening.

There are fewer emergency sequencing decisions.

Fewer recurring shortfalls converting into new balances.

Less dependence on perfect timing.

Less fragility around minor disruptions.

More visible operating margin.

More survivable repayment rhythm.

The household still manages money, of course. But the system no longer requires maximum attention every moment simply to preserve continuity.

This distinction is important because many households unconsciously assume that financial stability means becoming permanently more disciplined, more alert, more restrictive, or more intense indefinitely.

But durable systems usually move in the opposite direction.

They require less constant intervention over time.

A fragile structure depends heavily on ongoing coordination because small mistakes carry large consequences.

A stable structure contains enough margin and absorption capacity that ordinary human variability becomes survivable.

This is why repayment design matters so much.

A system depending entirely on relentless attention may improve temporarily while remaining operationally exhausting underneath. A system designed around survivability gradually reduces the pressure associated with maintaining progress.

The goal is not permanent financial hyper-vigilance.

The goal is a structure that remains functional even when attention fluctuates somewhat, conditions change, or ordinary life interrupts ideal coordination.

This does not mean repayment becomes effortless.

Long timelines still require patience. Obligations still remain active for periods of time. Improvement may still feel gradual.

But sustainable systems change the quality of the pressure.

The household no longer experiences every irregularity as a potential structural threat.

A repair becomes manageable disruption rather than immediate reversal.

A delayed paycheck becomes timing pressure rather than cascading instability.

An unexpected expense becomes absorbable rather than structurally destabilizing.

This changes the operating experience significantly even before all balances disappear entirely.

Control depletion weakens when the system itself becomes more survivable.

And survivability matters because repayment unfolds inside ordinary life, not outside it.

The household must continue functioning while repayment occurs.

Children still require care. Transportation still matters. Work schedules still fluctuate. Health issues still appear. Expenses still vary. Attention still shifts between competing responsibilities.

A repayment structure that survives only under ideal conditions is not stable enough for long-duration operation.

This is why debt stability cannot rely entirely on intensity.

Intensity fades.

Conditions change.

Attention fluctuates.

The structure itself must eventually carry more of the stabilization burden.

That is the deeper role of repayment sustainability.

Not slower repayment for its own sake.

Not comfort for its own sake.

But survivable progress.

Progress that continues even when energy levels are imperfect. Progress that survives ordinary disruption. Progress that does not collapse every time life behaves like real life instead of an idealized repayment spreadsheet.

Long repayment periods therefore require more than willingness.

They require structures that preserve control capacity across time.

Because the real goal is not maintaining permanent financial intensity indefinitely.

The goal is building a household system stable enough that control survives even when attention, energy, and conditions inevitably fluctuate.

From Payoff to Prevention

A falling balance can feel like the end of debt pressure.

Monthly obligations shrink. Statements become smaller. Minimum payments decline. More income remains available after recurring obligations are covered. The household begins experiencing space that did not previously exist.

This change matters. Reduced obligation load improves flexibility. Runway expands. Timing pressure weakens. Liquidity becomes easier to preserve. Recovery capacity improves.

But payoff alone does not automatically create long-term debt stability.

Balances can decline while the underlying structure that produced debt pressure remains largely unchanged.

A household may still operate with thin liquidity. Irregular expenses may still remain weakly absorbed. Baseline operating costs may still drift upward gradually. Income timing may still conflict with recurring obligations. Visibility may still weaken once immediate pressure fades.

This is why debt stability extends beyond repayment itself.

Post-Debt Governance is the ongoing review and maintenance of the household financial system after balances fall so debt pressure does not quietly rebuild.

The important distinction is that governance is not constant anxiety.

It is not permanent restriction.

It is not obsessive monitoring.

Governance is periodic visibility and correction.

A stable system does not require constant emergency attention. But it does require enough awareness to notice when pressure begins rebuilding before instability becomes severe again.

This matters because debt pressure rarely returns all at once.

Most rebuilding occurs gradually.

A financing plan for a replacement purchase appears manageable. A recurring subscription continues unnoticed. A temporary balance remains active longer than expected. A higher monthly service cost becomes normalized. An automatic draft continues operating quietly in the background. A period of improved income supports higher recurring obligations that later remain after conditions change.

Individually, these developments may appear insignificant.

Collectively, they alter the operating structure.

This gradual rebuilding process is important because households often associate debt instability with dramatic events. But many unstable structures develop through accumulation rather than collapse.

Pressure expands incrementally.

One new obligation rarely destabilizes the household alone.

The structure drifts.

This is one reason payoff can create a misleading sense of finality.

A household may eliminate balances successfully while assuming the system now permanently stabilizes automatically afterward. But debt pressure is not governed solely by whether balances currently exist. It is governed by how future obligations interact with liquidity, operating margin, timing coordination, and recovery capacity over time.

A household with no revolving balances but weak reserves, rising baseline costs, and recurring financing dependence may still remain structurally vulnerable to future debt regeneration.

The issue is not whether debt previously existed.

The issue is whether the operating structure now prevents pressure from rebuilding quietly underneath ordinary life.

This is where governance becomes important.

Governance means periodically observing whether the structure still fits the household's actual operating conditions.

Liquidity matters here.

As balances decline, households often redirect attention entirely toward payoff completion while underestimating the importance of preserving reserve capacity afterward. But liquidity continues functioning as shock absorption even after repayment improves.

Repairs still occur.

Income timing still shifts.

Medical expenses still appear.

Appliances still fail.

Administrative errors still happen.

Travel disruptions still emerge.

Without sufficient reserve flexibility, ordinary instability can still convert into future obligations later, even after significant repayment progress previously occurred.

This is one reason post-debt stability depends heavily on preserving liquidity rather than treating liquidity only as a temporary repayment-stage concern.

Protective reserves do not become irrelevant simply because balances fall.

If anything, their role becomes easier to recognize once obligation pressure weakens enough for the household to observe the difference between absorbable disruption and debt-generating disruption more clearly.

A vehicle repair handled directly through available liquidity behaves very differently from one financed through future obligations.

The repair itself may be identical.

The structural outcome is not.

The first disruption passes.

The second remains active afterward through recurring repayment pressure.

This distinction remains important long after earlier balances disappear.

Governance therefore includes noticing whether the household still possesses enough accessible flexibility to absorb ordinary instability without immediately recreating obligation pressure again.

Baseline drift matters equally.

One of the quietest forms of pressure rebuilding occurs when freed cash flow gradually disappears into higher operating costs.

A household reduces a recurring payment, then absorbs the available margin into upgraded services, higher convenience spending, recurring subscriptions, financed replacements, or elevated housing costs. None of these changes necessarily appear excessive individually. In many cases, they feel normal.

The problem is not the existence of comfort or improvement.

The issue is whether newly available flexibility becomes fully recommitted before resilience has time to strengthen underneath.

This process often develops invisibly because the household experiences improvement and expansion simultaneously.

A balance disappears.

Cash flow improves.

A higher recurring cost appears manageable because the prior payment no longer exists.

Then another obligation appears later.

Then another.

Over time, the operating threshold rises again.

The household may technically remain functional while gradually returning toward tighter margins and higher obligation density without fully recognizing the shift while it develops.

This is why governance includes observing whether reduced obligations are actually increasing flexibility or merely being replaced by new recurring commitments.

The distinction matters because restored flexibility is one of the primary structural benefits of debt reduction.

If every improvement in cash flow immediately converts into new fixed operating pressure, long-term resilience remains limited even when balances change.

Governance therefore protects not only against debt accumulation itself, but against the gradual erosion of regained adaptability.

Recurring obligation growth also deserves attention after repayment improves.

New financing structures often enter household systems quietly.

A replacement appliance becomes a payment plan. A furniture purchase becomes installment financing. A recurring service renews automatically. A deferred-payment structure extends beyond its expected period. A revolving balance remains active temporarily but never fully resolves.

None of these developments necessarily represent crisis conditions individually.

The problem is density.

As obligations layer together, future income becomes increasingly assigned again before it arrives.

This recreates many earlier forms of pressure:

timing coordination,
reduced liquidity rebuilding,
narrower operating margin,
higher disruption sensitivity,
and renewed obligation compression.

The household may not notice the shift immediately because the progression occurs gradually.

This is why periodic visibility matters.

Not obsession.

Visibility.

The system should remain understandable enough that recurring obligations do not accumulate silently for long periods without recognition.

Debt mapping remains relevant here even after balances decline substantially.

Earlier in the book, mapping clarified how fragmented obligations create pressure that becomes difficult to interpret clearly. That insight remains important afterward because fragmentation often returns quietly once urgency fades.

Automatic drafts continue operating.

Subscriptions continue renewing.

Installment structures continue extending.

Recurring services continue layering.

Governance means periodically bringing the structure back into visibility before accumulated pressure becomes normalized again.

The purpose is not perfection.

The purpose is early correction.

A stable household does not avoid every future mistake, unexpected cost, or inefficient decision forever. Real systems remain imperfect because life remains variable.

Governance matters because small adjustments made early are usually easier to absorb than large corrections delayed too long.

A household noticing rising baseline costs early may adjust gradually without disruption.

A household recognizing weakening liquidity early may slow new obligation growth before instability intensifies.

A household observing recurring timing pressure early may realign obligations before coordination strain escalates further.

These are not dramatic interventions.

They are maintenance corrections.

This is one reason governance should feel calm rather than punitive.

The goal is not constant self-surveillance.

The goal is preserving enough visibility that drift remains detectable before pressure becomes urgent again.

A well-governed structure therefore behaves differently from a reactive structure.

Reactive systems notice pressure only after instability becomes difficult to absorb.

Governed systems notice changes earlier because the household remains connected to how the structure is functioning operationally over time.

This distinction reduces the likelihood that debt pressure rebuilds invisibly for years before recognition occurs.

Income timing still matters here as well.

A household may improve substantially during one income phase while slowly becoming mismatched again later as schedules change, commissions fluctuate, overtime declines, or recurring obligations expand beyond what the current flow structure comfortably supports.

Governance includes periodically observing whether obligations still fit the household's real operating rhythm rather than assuming prior alignment automatically remains stable indefinitely.

The same applies to repayment capacity.

A structure that once supported aggressive reduction may not support the same pressure later if conditions change. Conversely, a structure previously too fragile for faster repayment may later become more resilient as liquidity improves and obligations decline.

Governance therefore remains adaptive rather than rigid.

The household continues interpreting the structure as conditions evolve.

This adaptability matters because stable systems are rarely static.

Expenses change.

Income changes.

Household size changes.

Responsibilities change.

Operating conditions shift across time.

The objective is not freezing the system permanently.

The objective is maintaining enough awareness that changes remain manageable instead of silently destabilizing.

Toward the later stages of repayment, another subtle risk sometimes appears.

Fatigue weakens visibility.

After long periods of pressure, households understandably want relief from constant financial attention. Once balances decline meaningfully, there can be a strong desire to stop monitoring the structure closely altogether.

This reaction is understandable.

But complete disengagement may allow obligation layering, baseline drift, or liquidity erosion to rebuild gradually without correction.

The solution is not permanent intensity.

The solution is lighter but ongoing governance.

A stable system eventually requires less attention than a fragile one. But less attention is not the same as no attention at all.

Governance becomes quieter over time.

Less emergency coordination.

Less crisis management.

Less constant sequencing pressure.

More periodic review.

More gentle correction.

More preserved flexibility.

The structure gradually shifts from reactive stabilization toward ongoing maintenance.

That transition matters because the household is no longer operating only to survive immediate pressure. It is now preserving the conditions that prevent pressure from rebuilding repeatedly in the future.

Near this stage, many forms of instability become easier to recognize earlier than before.

A recurring service expansion now appears differently because the household understands obligation layering more clearly.

A financing plan now appears differently because the household recognizes future income assignment more clearly.

A thin liquidity position now appears differently because the household understands shock conversion more clearly.

This accumulated visibility is one of the most valuable outcomes of debt stabilization.

Not fear.

Interpretation.

The household no longer sees debt only as balances.

It sees the structure that produces pressure underneath them.

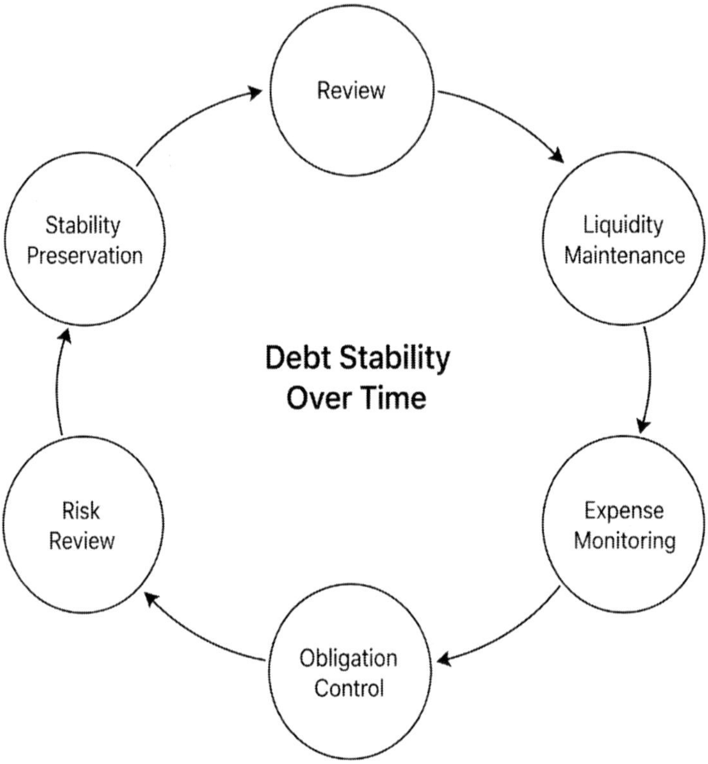

[Figure 10: Post-Debt Governance Loop]

Governance therefore becomes less about reacting to emergencies and more about preserving flexibility before emergencies become destabilizing again.

A stable household still experiences disruption. It still encounters repairs, irregular costs, timing shifts, and changing conditions. But the structure becomes more capable of absorbing those changes without automatically converting them into renewed obligation pressure.

That distinction is the deeper meaning of debt stability.

Not permanent perfection.

Not permanent intensity.

Not the absence of all future borrowing forever.

Debt stability is the household's ability to prevent obligation pressure from quietly rebuilding after progress has already been made.

Control Returns Gradually

Debt pressure rarely appears all at once.

In many households, it develops gradually through recurring obligations, timing strain, liquidity weakness, irregular expenses, and the slow assignment of future income before that income arrives. A balance grows. A payment becomes recurring. Flexibility narrows. Coordination becomes harder. More of the household's operating capacity becomes committed before ordinary life even begins each month.

The pressure accumulates quietly.

Because of this, debt stability rarely returns all at once either.

It returns gradually.

Not through one payment.

Not through one decision.

Not through intensity alone.

It returns as pressure weakens and flexibility begins reappearing inside the structure again.

That distinction shaped the purpose of this book from the beginning.

Debt was never treated here as a moral category or a personal failure. The goal was not to divide households into responsible and irresponsible groups, nor to frame debt as evidence of discipline or weakness. The goal was to make debt pressure visible as an operating condition that affects liquidity, timing, recovery capacity, flexibility, and the household's ability to absorb ordinary instability.

Debt changes how future income behaves.

Income that might otherwise rebuild reserves, absorb disruption, or restore flexibility becomes partially assigned in advance through recurring obligations. Minimum payments continue arriving. Interest extends timelines. Timing pressure narrows operating margin. The household becomes more dependent on uninterrupted continuity because less room remains available for error or interruption.

Over time, debt therefore behaves less like a static balance and more like an active pressure system.

That pressure affects more than repayment itself.

It affects runway.

A household carrying dense recurring obligations usually possesses less financial time under disruption than a household operating with lower obligation pressure. Repairs, income delays, medical expenses, irregular costs, and timing shifts become more destabilizing when little liquidity exists underneath the structure.

This is why debt pressure often feels immediate even when income technically appears sufficient across longer periods.

The issue is frequently not total income alone.

The issue is whether the household possesses enough flexibility to absorb ordinary instability without continuously converting disruption into future obligations.

Many of the systems explored throughout this book emerge from that single reality.

Debt compresses runway because recurring obligations continue consuming resources even when conditions weaken temporarily. Payment tolerance narrows because dense obligations reduce adaptability. Accumulation drag extends instability timelines because interest, fees, and revolving balances slow recovery even while repayment continues. Flow misalignment intensifies pressure when rigid obligations collide with irregular income timing. Substitution pressure develops when recurring shortfalls repeatedly shift toward borrowed capacity.

Over time, these pressures interact.

Shock conversion turns ordinary instability into long-term repayment obligations when liquidity cannot absorb disruption directly. Baseline inflation raises operating thresholds gradually as financed expansion becomes normalized. Fragmented obligations become harder to interpret clearly without visibility into the entire structure. Maintenance traps preserve account continuity without necessarily restoring flexibility underneath.

The deeper pattern connecting all of these mechanisms is relatively simple.

Debt pressure grows when the household loses its ability to absorb ordinary life cleanly.

That is why stability improves through reduction in fragility rather than repayment intensity alone.

Throughout the book, debt reduction was framed not as an emotional contest, but as a structural process. Repayment matters. But repayment becomes unstable when it destroys operating margin, weakens liquidity, or assumes conditions that ordinary household life rarely sustains consistently.

This is why repayment capacity matters.

A household may technically be able to direct more money toward balances temporarily while simultaneously making the structure more vulnerable to disruption. Without enough remaining flexibility, one repair, timing shift, or interruption may erase months of progress.

The problem is not lack of effort.

The problem is that repayment must survive ordinary instability long enough for stability to accumulate gradually.

This is also why reducing new debt formation matters as much as reducing existing balances.

Repayment alone cannot stabilize a structure that continuously regenerates new obligations underneath the payoff process itself. Leakage interruption matters because recurring shortfalls, timing gaps, irregular costs, and weak liquidity repeatedly recreate borrowing pressure if the operating system underneath remains unstable.

The same principle applies to obligation alignment.

Debt pressure is experienced not only through balances, but through timing. A payment structure that fits poorly inside the household's actual cash-flow rhythm creates unnecessary coordination strain even when obligations appear manageable on paper. Alignment reduces avoidable instability by making repayment more survivable inside ordinary life conditions.

Protective liquidity serves a similar role.

A household with no reserve capacity may remain technically committed to repayment while still remaining highly vulnerable to reversal. Small buffers matter because ordinary instability continues occurring throughout repayment periods. Repairs still happen. Delays still happen. Expenses still cluster unexpectedly. Liquidity allows disruption to remain temporary rather than becoming renewed obligation pressure.

Even repayment sequencing ultimately depends on structural interpretation rather than ideology.

Different obligations create different forms of instability. Some compress liquidity aggressively. Some create timing congestion. Some extend accumulation drag. Some threaten continuity more directly. Sequencing becomes more effective when it reduces the household's actual pressure profile rather than simply following universal formulas detached from the structure itself.

Over long timelines, another reality becomes visible as well.

Debt pressure affects attention.

Control depletion develops because prolonged repayment periods require sustained coordination across months or years. The household continues managing timing, obligations, liquidity, irregular expenses, and operating pressure long after initial urgency fades. Fatigue emerges not necessarily because progress is absent, but because the structure still demands continuous attention while improvement remains gradual.

This is one reason stable systems eventually aim to reduce control load itself.

A healthier structure requires less constant emergency coordination over time. Fewer disruptions convert into balances. Timing becomes less fragile. Liquidity absorbs more instability directly. Repayment becomes less dependent on perfect conditions or maximum intensity indefinitely.

Eventually, stability becomes visible in ordinary ways.

More margin remains after recurring obligations.

Fewer emergencies become long-term balances.

Payment timing feels less chaotic.

Recovery after disruption becomes faster.

Decisions become clearer because fewer pressures compete simultaneously.

The household spends less time coordinating survival and more time operating normally.

This shift is often quieter than people expect.

Stability rarely arrives as a dramatic moment.

More often, it appears through reduced fragility.

A repair no longer creates immediate panic.

A delayed paycheck no longer destabilizes the month automatically.

An irregular expense no longer requires immediate borrowing.

A balance that once remained permanently active finally resolves and stays resolved.

Pressure weakens gradually enough that the household sometimes notices the absence of instability before noticing the presence of stability itself.

That change matters because the ultimate goal was never simply balance elimination in isolation.

Balances can disappear temporarily while the underlying conditions that produced debt pressure remain active. Without governance, baseline drift can quietly return. New obligations can layer gradually. Liquidity can weaken again. Timing strain can rebuild silently underneath improving income periods.

Debt stability therefore continues after payoff.

Not through constant fear or obsessive monitoring, but through ongoing visibility into whether the structure still preserves flexibility, liquidity, timing stability, and interruption capacity.

A stable household is not one where nothing ever goes wrong.

Repairs still happen.

Income still changes.

Unexpected costs still appear.

Ordinary life remains variable.

The difference is that ordinary instability no longer automatically becomes future obligation pressure every time conditions shift.

That is the deeper meaning of debt stability.

Not perfect behavior.

Not permanent intensity.

Not the complete absence of all future borrowing under every condition.

Debt stability is the rebuilding of a household system capable of meeting ordinary life without repeatedly borrowing from the future.

About the Author

Mark Ellison writes about financial stability in systems exposed to pressure, uncertainty, and time.

His work examines how household financial capacity is shaped by liquidity, income flow, expense control, debt pressure, risk exposure, decision quality, and governance. Rather than treating budgeting, saving, debt reduction, and investing as isolated tactics, he approaches them as interacting financial systems governed by margin, timing, constraint, exposure, and control.

The Stability framework explores how financial compression accumulates gradually and how durable structure preserves long-horizon flexibility across changing economic conditions. The objective is not wealth performance alone, but preservation of financial control under load.

Debt Stability is part of a broader money stability ecosystem developed under Perennial Publishing, each volume addressing a distinct vector of financial durability.

The work is designed for readers who prefer structural clarity over motivational rhetoric and long-horizon coherence over short-term financial intensity.

The Money Stability Series

Money Stability
Liquidity and Runway
Income Stability
Expense Stability
Risk Stability
Financial Decisions
Governance Stability

Debt Stability

Part of a Broader Stability Framework

The Money Stability Series is part of a larger stability ecosystem published by Perennial Publishing.

Related domains include:

Metabolic Stability — biological load, energy, and recovery capacity

Career Stability — income durability, positioning, and transition resilience

Mental Stability — cognitive steadiness under pressure and uncertainty

Emotional Stability — regulatory steadiness in environments that do not slow down

Each domain approaches stability as a structural problem: capacity versus load, buffers versus shocks, and governance versus drift. Together, they form a unified framework for long-horizon durability across the major systems that determine life trajectory.

About Perennial Publishing

Perennial Publishing produces practical systems guides for building stability in an unstable world.

Our books explore the foundations of long-term resilience across health, finance, career, and everyday decision-making. Each title focuses on clear frameworks, durable principles, and practical strategies that help readers build lasting stability rather than short-term fixes.

The Perennial catalog includes series on metabolic health, financial stability, career systems, and personal consistency. While each book stands on its own, they share a common goal: helping individuals create durable systems that support a stable and sustainable life.

For bulk or institutional orders, contact Perennial Publishing at: orders@perennialpublishing.org

Made in United States
North Haven, CT
04 November 2026

21768639R00118